KT-153-793

Lanzarote
& Fuerteventura

by Andrew Sanger

Andrew Sanger is a well-established travel
journalist who has contributed to a wide
range of popular magazines and most British
newspapers. He is the author of more than
twenty travel guides, including *Essential
Tenerife, TwinPack Tenerife, TwinPack
Lanzarote & Fuerteventura* and *Explorer Israel*
for the AA. He has twice won at the annual
Travelex Travel Writers' Awards.

Above: Playa de Papagayo, Lanzarote

AA Publishing

Lace-making at Bodega Santa Maria

Written and updated by Andrew Sanger

First published 1999
Reprinted 2001, verified and updated. Reprinted May 2001, Feb 2002
Second edition 2002. Reprinted 2004
Reprinted 2005. Information verified and updated.
Reprinted May and Aug 2005
Reprinted Jan and Apr 2006
Reprinted Feb and July 2007

© Automobile Association Developments Limited 2002

Published by AA Publishing, a trading name of Automobile Association Developments Limited, whose registered office is at Fanum House, Basing View, Basingstoke, Hampshire, RG21 4EA. Registered number 1878835.

Automobile Association Developments Limited retains the copyright in the original edition © 1999 and in all subsequent editions, reprints and amendments.

A CIP catalogue record for this book is available from the British Library.

All rights reserved. No part of this publication may be reproduced, stored in a retrieval system, or transmitted in any form or by any means – electronic, photocopying, recording or otherwise – unless the written permission of the publishers has been obtained beforehand. This book may not be sold, resold, hired out or otherwise disposed of by way of trade in any form of binding or cover other than that in which it is published, without the prior consent of the publisher.
    The contents of this publication are believed correct at the time of printing. Nevertheless, AA Publishing accept no responsibility for errors or omissions or changes in the details given, or for the consequences of readers' reliance on this information. This does not affect your statutory rights. Assessments of attractions, hotels and restaurants are based upon the author's own experience and contain subjective opinions that may not reflect the publisher's opinion or a reader's experience. We have tried to ensure accuracy in this guide, but things do change so please let us know if you have any comments or corrections.

Find out more about AA Publishing and the wide range of travel publications and services the AA provides by visiting our website at www.theAA.com/travel

A03510

Colour separation: Keenes, Andover
Printed and bound in Italy by Printer Trento S.r.l.

Contents

About this Book

KEY TO SYMBOLS

✚ grid reference to the maps found in the What to See section

✉ address or location

☎ telephone number

🕐 opening times

🍴 restaurant or café on premises or near by

🚇 nearest underground train station

🚌 nearest bus/tram route

🚉 nearest overground train station

🚢 ferry crossings and boat excursions

✈ travel by air

ℹ tourist information

♿ facilities for visitors with disabilities

✋ admission charge

↔ other places of interest near by

❓ other practical information

➤ indicates the page where you will find a fuller description

This book is divided into five sections to cover the most important aspects of your visit to the islands.

Viewing Lanzarote & Fuerteventura
pages 5–14
An introduction to the islands by the author.
   Features of Lanzarote & Fuerteventura
   Essence of Lanzarote & Fuerteventura
   The Shaping of Lanzarote & Fuerteventura
   Peace and Quiet
   Famous of Lanzarote & Fuerteventura

Top Ten pages 15–26
The author's choice of the Top Ten places to see on the islands, listed in alphabetical order, each with practical information.

What to See pages 27–90
The islands of Lanzarote & Fuerteventura, each with its own brief introduction and an alphabetical listing of the main attractions.
   Practical information
   Snippets of 'Did you know…' information
   4 suggested walks
   5 suggested tours
   3 features

Where To… pages 91–116
Detailed listings of the best places to eat, stay, shop, take the children and be entertained.

Practical Matters pages 117–124
A highly visual section containing essential travel information.

Maps
All map references are to the individual maps found in the What to See section of this guide.
For example, Islote de Hilario has the reference ✚ 28B2 – indicating the page on which the map is located and the grid square in which the mountain is to be found. A list of the maps that have been used in this travel guide can be found in the index.

Prices
Where appropriate, an indication of the cost of an establishment is given by € signs:

€€€ denotes higher prices, €€ denotes average prices, while € denotes lower charges.

Star Ratings
Most of the places described in this book have been given a separate rating:

000 Do not miss
00 Highly recommended
0 Worth seeing

Viewing
Lanzarote
& Fuerteventura

Above: *Fuerteventura is a world
centre for windsurfing*
Right: *basket-weaving in
Fuerteventura*

Andrew Sanger's
Lanzarote & Fuerteventura

A Long Way From Spain
Though Spanish, Lanzarote and Fuerteventura are much nearer to the Sahara than to Spain. These two most easterly of the Canary Islands are only around 96km from the coast of Africa. Lanzarote is the most northerly of the Canaries. Lanzarote and Fuerteventura possess four smaller isles; Lobos, La Graciosa, Alegranza and Montaña Clara.

There's something in the harsh paradox of these volcanic islands that thrills the soul. The austere, timeless emptiness; the dryness recalling the nearby Sahara; the menacing hint of nature's enduring power, the over-whelming solitude and silence – all these beckon, yet defy man to make a home here.

These islands are indeed very thinly populated. Fuerteventura's average of 11 people per square kilometre is the lowest in the Canaries, and even that figure gives no clue to the sense of space, for almost everyone lives in just one place – Puerto del Rosario. Lanzarote's case, while not quite as extreme, is similar: most people live in Arrecife.

Yet these are not desert islands, but Spanish territories with agriculture, art, history, traditions and folkore, culture and cuisine. They are also holiday lands with hotels, beaches, satellite TV and hire cars.

That is the paradox. The destructive forces of nature – exemplified by the eruption of Timanfaya volcano in the 1730s, when burning rock rained on Lanzarote and swept away fields and villages that islanders had nurtured for centuries – have themselves now been harnessed by man's own great powers of survival and imagination. Getting visitors to pay to see the volcanoes, and using the heat of the Fire Mountains to barbecue steaks, is a victory of sorts. A temporary one, perhaps, for the volcanoes may erupt again one day, and the sands continue to blow over from Africa.

The enticing main beach of Puerto del Carmen, Lanzarote

Features of Lanzarote & Fuerteventura

People
• Some 115,000 people live on Lanzarote and about 60,000 on Fuerteventura. On both islands, over half the population live in their respective capital.
• Ethnically the islanders are thought to be a mix of Berber, Arab, Norman and Spanish.
• Fuerteventura natives are known as *maioreros*, while Lanzeroteños are called *conejos*, meaning rabbits.

A Tropical Wind
Nearly all of Lanzarote and Fuerteventura's holiday accommodation is on the south-facing coasts, which are sheltered from the prevailing trade winds (*alisios*, in Spanish). Trade winds, found only in tropical regions, blow from the northwest. Lying between the 28th and 29th parallels, Lanzarote and Fuerteventura are less than 645km from the Tropic of Cancer.

Left: *a Lanzaroteño takes time to reflect*

Climate
• Unlike the other Canaries, these two islands remain practically rain-free all year round, though there can be winter cloud. Any rain that does fall normally comes between October and March, and falls on an average of only 16 days per year, with a total annual precipitation of about 138mm.
• Average daytime temperatures remain almost constant at around 20°C on Lanzarote, 19°C on Fuerteventura all year round.
• Both islands can be windy, especially on the western sides.

Size
• The second largest of the Canaries, Fuerteventura is only slightly smaller than Tenerife. At 1,731sq km, it is over twice the size of Lanzarote's 813sq km.

Language
• Spanish is the language of the Canaries, but islanders also have a patois of their own. English is widely spoken (though not usually very well), especially at resorts and tourist attractions.

Right: *Lanzarote still blooms despite the lack of rain*

Essence of Lanzarote & Fuerteventura

Awesome dunes run along the coast of northeast Fuerteventura

Most people visiting these two most easterly of the Canary Islands are looking for sun, sea, sand and sights; but look too for earth, wind and fire. Over the millennia, these powerful natural forces have given Lanzarote and Fuerteventura their distinctive character: dramatic volcanic land-scapes, waterless – but not barren – hills, and gorgeous beaches of pure Sahara sand are the impressive legacies.

These islands have avoided the overdevel-opment and 'lager lout' culture of many other popular sunshine destinations. Low-key family resorts, well-equipped small complexes, inland villas with pools, and an unspoiled blue and gold coastline give Lanzarote and Fuerteventura a civilised air.

THE **10** ESSENTIALS

If you only have a short time to visit Lanzarote and Fuerteventura, or would like to get a complete picture of the islands, here are the essentials:

• **See twigs burst into flame** on Islote de Hilario. The scorching ground temperature ignites brushwood and boils water in seconds (➤ 20–21).
• **Take the bus tour** from Islote de Hilario. It's the only way to get into the very heart of volcano country.
• **Visit the Fundación César Manrique**. The genius and flair of the man who made Lanzarote great can be felt in his former home (➤ 19), which is now an important art gallery.
• **Go to the Jameos del Agua** during the day just to gaze and wonder, or in the evening for a night out in an amazing setting (➤ 22).
• **Eat *papas arrugadas con mojo***. These ultra-tasty, salty new potatoes are one of the best local specialities (➤ 82–83). *Mojo* is a traditional Canarian piquant sauce.
• **Drink Lanzarote wine**. If you think a barren volcanic landscape is not the best place to grow grapes, you haven't tried Lanzarote's cool, crisp and dry Malvasia white wines.
• **Sunbathe on a golden beach**, not the grainy black stuff more typical of the other Canaries. Lanzarote and Fuerteventura have long, wide stretches of fine pale sands.
• **Walk ten paces on the *malpaís***. To understand just how unworkable this land is, try walking on it. The best place to try this is La Geria (➤ 26), where it's easy to

pull over to the side of the road and get out of the car.
• **Walk on giant sand dunes**. East of Lanzarote's Playa Blanca, or in Fuerteventura's Dunes Natural Park or Pared Isthmus, stroll on the rolling, drifting desert sandscapes.
• **Take a trip to another island**. Whether you're on Lanzarote or Fuerteventura, it's worth making a day trip to see the sights of the other. It's also fun to visit Isla Graciosa (off Lanzarote) or Isla de Lobos (off Fuerteventura).

Timanfaya's volcanic heat ignites brushwood in no time

Playa de Sotavento, Fuerteventura

The Shaping of Lanzarote & Fuerteventura

17–20 million years ago
Huge volcanic eruptions create Fuerteventura and Lanzarote.

2000–2500 BC
The islands are occupied by the Guanches, a tall, white race, thought to have been Berbers from north Africa; they speak a language recognisably related to that of the Berbers.

82 BC
Roman sailors visit the two eastern Canary Islands. Greek and Roman tradition refers to the Canaries as the Fortunate Isles.

CAD 1
Juba II of Mauretania

Jean de Béthencourt

sends an expedition to explore the Fortunate Isles. All the islands are then named, one of them being called Canaria on account of its wild dogs (Latin *canis*, dog).

CAD 1000
Arab raiders pay a first visit, taking a few Guanche slaves; they call the islands Kaledat.

1312
Genoese sailor Lancelotto Malocello visits Fuerteventura and Lanzarote (which is a corruption of his name).

1339
Mallorcan cartographer Angelino Dolcet draws the first map showing the Canaries, though he only includes Fuerteventura and Lanzarote.

1341
A Genoese expedition reports that Fuerteventura (and perhaps Lanzarote) is covered in goats and trees.

1350–1450
Assorted raiders and slavers pause at the islands to capture slaves.

1402
Two Normans, Gadifer de la Salle and Jean de Béthencourt, land on Lanzarote, basing themselves on the Rubicón coastline (west of Playa Blanca). They claim the islands for the king of Spain.

1405
Jean de Béthencourt and de la Salle establish a first settlement on Fuerteventura at Betancuría and begin the process of colonisation.

Early 1400s
Norman and Spanish settlers enslave the Guanches and build European-style farming villages.

1400–1500
French, English, Dutch and Arab pirates raid both islands, capturing both Guanche and mixed-blood slaves. Most are sold at Valencia, in Spain.

1730–36
Timanfaya eruptions destroy a third of Lanzarote. Many islanders flee to Europe and South America.

1824
New volcanic eruptions add to the destruction and the layer of *malpaís*.

1919
César Manrique is born in Arrecife, Lanzarote. As a young man he leaves to study art in Madrid.

1924
Don Miguel Unamuno is exiled to Fuerteventura, and praises its harsh simplicty.

1940s
Fascist Spain is believed to use southern Fuerteventura to assist Nazis.

Early 1960s
Package tourism to the Canaries begins.

1968
César Manrique returns to Lanzarote and completes his first major landscape work, Jameos del Agua. Timanfaya is set aside as a protected natural area, and limitations are placed on its development.

1970
Timanfaya begins to receive tourists, and Manrique opens El Diablo restaurant.

1970–77
The period of César Manrique's prolific landscape and conservation work on Lanzarote. Most of his great Lanzarote 'landscape and tourism' projects were completed at this time.

1974
The Spanish Government declares Timanfaya a National Park, to be strictly protected.

A 300-year-old map of the Canary Islands

1978
Manrique receives the World Ecology and Tourism Award.

1986
Manrique receives the Europa Nostra Award for conservation work on Lanzarote.

1990
Jardín de Cactus, the last of Manrique's tourist attractions, is completed.

1992
César Manrique is killed in a car accident at the Tahíche junction, on 25 September.

1993
The Corralejo dunes on Fuerteventura are made a Natural Park. UNESCO declares the whole island of Lanzarote a world biosphere reserve.

Peace & Quiet

It's hard *not* to get away from it all on Lanzarote, while on Fuerteventura it's even easier to escape the crowd. The tourist industry on both islands is confined to a small number of resorts, with huge areas of unspoiled countryside, dunes, beaches and volcanic *malpaís* all within a short distance.

Exploring

Use the road map from Lanzarote's tourist offices to find minor roads and tracks (some are in very poor condition) leading into the heart of deserted island scenery or down to empty beaches and bays. Or leave the crowd behind just by walking away along the long sandy beaches and rocky coasts.

Fuerteventura, too, is crossed by minor tracks and trails where neither tourists nor locals are much seen. With a four-wheel-drive, follow tracks on the Jandía Peninsula to beautiful, lonely sands. Beware, though, of swimming in such lonely places, especially on the west coast of Fuerteventura, as undercurrents can be dangerous.

Nature Reserves

Both islands have large protected zones where development has been forbidden, and where distinctive flora and fauna can be spotted. In fact, despite the seemingly barren landscape, Lanzarote and Fuerteventura are a haven for certain rare plants and birds and even harbour several native species unique to these two islands.

Lanzarote's offshore island, La Graciosa, though easily accessible by ferry from Orzola, is a place to find perfect solitude. The other, more remote islands, Montaña Clara and Alegranza, are breeding grounds for little shearwaters and Bulwer's petrels. In northern Lanzarote, the almost deserted sands of Famara beach are backed by rugged 700m cliffs, where Eleonora's falcons breed.

Lanzarote's cacti were cultivated for cochineal beetles to live on

On and below the cliffs, yellow-flowering *Pulicaria canariensis* fleabane, *Argyranthemum ochroleucum*, looking like an unkempt ragwort, and the pretty yellow daisy bush *Astericus schultzii* flourish: all are unique to Lanzarote and Fuerteventura. On the clifftop grows *Ferula lancerottensis*, the umbellifer also unique to this location. You'll see, too, attractive Canarian varieties of the euphorbia succulents, which positively thrive around the islands' coasts, such as the swollen-stemmed *Euphorbia canariensis*.

Inland, the Famara heights descend into the lush Haría valley, where a gentle micro-climate creates a miniature world of flourishing palms, cacti and several unique species of plant.

Did you know ?

*Surprisingly, that well-known, bright
yellow songbird called* Serinus canaria *is not
seen here. The Canaries are not named after
the birds, as some believe, but the other way
round. The islands were called after quite a
different native – wild dogs (the Latin* canis *means
dog), probably those found on Fuerteventura.
A white–pawed local breed still survives, the
descendant of the original inhabitants.*

*A lovely monarch butterfly
spotted at the Agricultural
Museum, Lanzarote*

Desertscapes

Fuerteventura's dry, barren, unpopulated landscapes and
the tracts of sand dunes are just the place to find peace
and quiet, and discover the low, clinging plants that can
live here. The sandy Jandía Peninsula gives its name to the
red-flowered cactus-like *Euphorbia handiensis* succulent,
found only on these beaches. Climb the high slopes
behind to find the straggling blue-flowering *Echium
handiense* bugloss, also unique to this island.

On both islands, the houbara bustard, cream-coloured
courser and black-bellied sandgrouse – rare species
elsewhere – are at home in the dry, desert-like *malpaís* and
dunes. Several native birds seen here are paler versions of
their European cousins, for example the rare Canarian
chat, Berthelot's pipit and short-toed lark. You'll also see
the trumpeter finch, with its short red beak, and hear its
unmistakable call.

*Spectacular views of the
offshore islands to the
north of Lanzarote*

Famous of Lanzarote & Fuerteventura

Famous Visitors
King Hussein of Jordan once owned a holiday home on Lanzarote (since given to King Juan Carlos I of Spain). Taken to visit Manrique, King Hussein lit up a cigarette. Manrique asked him not to smoke, adding 'In this house, I am the king'.

Raquel Welch, dressed only in a fur bikini, can be seen in a desolate Timanfaya landscape in the film *One Million Years BC*.

Fuerteventura's most distinguished visitor was the poet and philosopher Unamuno, who was exiled there in 1924.

Fundación César Manrique is housed in the artist's former home

César Manrique

César Manrique (1919–92) was born in Arrecife and made Lanzarote famous. The local lad, whose genius made him an international figure in the world of modern art, actually left Lanzarote as a young man. He prospered in New York, Paris and Madrid, formed close friendships with his compatriots Picasso and Miró, and became an acclaimed modern artist.

He eventually returned home in 1968 to a hero's welcome. Manrique adored the island, and was fascinated by man's relationship with landscape. He was also intrigued by the mass tourism then taking off in the Canaries – its destructive power, and equally, the benefits it could bring. Manrique was eager to ensure that development took place with respect for local culture and tradition.

The regional council gave him a free hand to do whatever he wanted, and Lanzarote became Manrique's *atelier*. He laid down autocratic architectural rules. He banned all roadside billboards (take a look, there aren't any). He put up fantastic, wind-driven giant mobile sculptures at major crossroads. He took over Lanzarote's geographical oddities and with sheer brilliance turned them into extraordinary attractions.

Many of his ideas became law, including the rules that no new buildings may be more than two storeys (except in Arrecife and tourist zones) high, and that window shutters must be plain wood or green, except by the sea, where blue is allowed. While new coastal developments disregard some rules, there are still no high-rise hotels.

In 1978 Manrique received the World Ecology and Tourism Award, and in 1986 the Europa Nostra Award for conservation. In 1992, at the age of 74, César Manrique died in a car crash at the intersection near his home (which he had said for years was dangerous). He is buried at Haría, and today is regarded by the islanders almost in the light of a secular saint.

César Manrique © DACS, 1998

Top Ten

**Note: except for No 3,
all the Top Ten sights
are on Lanzarote**

Above: *street lighting in
Teguise*
Right: *a country islander
takes a break*

1
Castillo de San José

An important collection of modern art is housed in this beautiful little semicircular stone fortress on a clifftop overlooking the sea.

 29C2

 Puerto de Naos 3km north of Arrecife on the Muelle de los Mármoles road

928 81 23 21

 Museum: daily 11AM–9PM
Castle: daily 11AM–midnight

Restaurant (€€), bar (€)

 Every 30 mins from Arrecife waterfront, every hour at weekends and festivals

Blas Cabrera Felipe (by waterfront), Arrecife
928 81 17 62

Few

Free

Above: *the 'Hunger Fortress' now houses an art gallery and an imaginative modern restaurant*

The commanding position of San José Castle once made it a vital defence for the island's capital and port against the pirates who plagued the Canaries. Today it looks down on the busy commercial harbour of Puerto de Naos.

Built of black basalt in the midst of a period of great suffering after the eruption of Timanfaya, the castle came to be known as the Hunger Fortress. It is entered by crossing a moat, and the year of its completion, 1779, is carved above the entrance. Despite its strictly military purpose, the two-storey castle possesses great elegance and charm both inside and out. Its spacious halls and spiral stairwells, and the sharp contrast of black stone and white walls, create an atmosphere of powerful, stark simplicity. Floors are paved with patterned black volcanic slabs and black pebbles. The barrel-vaulted ceilings, too, are black.

In 1976 César Manrique restored the castle and installed the Museo Internacional de Arte Contemporáneo (International Museum of Contemporary Art) devoted to abstract modern art. The fantastic juxtaposition of vivid 20th-century forms and the black 18th-century fortress is startling, especially just inside the dark entrance, where a modern sculpture in glistening white marble stands. However, the paintings are poorly labelled and no catalogue is available.

Spiral steps lead down to César Manrique's own contribution, a glass-walled restaurant and bar overlooking the sea, with black tables, black napkins and modern classical music playing.

2
Cueva de los Verdes (Greens' Cave)

The guided 1km walk through part of one of the longest lava cave systems in the world is enhanced by lighting, music and natural illusions.

Monte Corona is an extinct volcano in northern Lanzarote, whose eruptions some 5,000 years ago created a *malpaís* – a contorted, blackened landscape similar to Timanfaya at the other end of the island. The Corona eruptions formed one of the world's longest lava caves, Cueva de los Verdes and neighbouring Jameos del Agua being part of the same 7.5km Corona system (of which 1.5km is beneath the seabed). These hollow tubes were carved out as older basalt rock was melted and washed away by the lava flowing around it, and underground gases inflated the molten terrain.

The network of caverns and tunnels has long been known to locals, who used to hide here during the 17th century when Arab slave hunters and pirates raided the island. Cueva de los Verdes (not in fact a 'green' cave – Verde was the family name of former owners) is a short section reached by descending to a tunnel below ground level. Hour-long guided visits in English take visitors along a circular 1km walkway, narrow and low-ceilinged in places. Haunting music and lighting heighten the experience, which takes in vividly coloured rocks, impressive rock formations and a clever optical illusion at the end of the tour.

The entrance and ticket booth to the caves have been discreetly arranged to avoid disfiguring the barren seashore *malpaís*, which can be explored on footpaths.

✚ 29D4

✉ 2km from Arrieta (26km north of Arrecife)

☎ 928 84 84 84

🕐 Daily 10–6 (last tour at 5)

🍴 Cheap fish restaurants (€) on Arrieta waterfront

🚌 No 9 (Arrecife-Orzola) passes about 1km away; three times a day Mon–Fri, twice a day Sat–Sun

ℹ Blas Cabrora Felipe (by waterfront), Arrecife ☎ 928 81 17 62

♿ None (unsuitable for anyone who cannot walk and bend with ease)

✋ Moderate

↔ Jameos del Agua (► 22)

Amazing rock formations inside the volcanic caves

3
Dunes of Fuerteventura

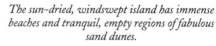

🏳️ 76C1, 77E5

🍴 Hotel Tres Islas has restaurants (€€) and bars. Restaurants (€–€€) in Corralejo. Also El Camello (€–€€) at La Pared

🚌 No 6 (Corralejo–Puerto del Rosario)

⛴️ To Corralejo from Playa Blanca on Lanzarote takes 24 minutes.

✈️ Airport just south of the Parque Natural

ℹ️ Plaza Grande, Corralejo ☎ 928 86 62 35; CC Shopping Center, Morro Jable ☎ 928 54 07 76

↔️ Corralejo (► 80), Isla de Lobos (► 84), La Oliva (► 87), Tarajalejo (► 90), Jandía Peninsula (► 84)

The dunes of Playa de Sotavento stretch for nearly 30km along the southern shore of the Jandía Peninsula

The sun-dried, windswept island has immense beaches and tranquil, empty regions of fabulous sand dunes.

Like a miniature Sahara, the island of Fuerteventura is sandy and waterless, windy and parched. For millennia sands have blown here across the 60 miles from Africa, covering the volcanic layer beneath, creating endless dune landscapes and great hills of pale sand.

Right behind Fuerteventura's main resort, Corralejo, on the island's northern tip, rises its largest and most impressive single area of dunes. This complex system of dazzling pale sands, stretching about 10km along the coast and reaching 2–3km inland from the shore, has been declared a protected zone known as the Parque Natural de las Dunas de Corralejo. Despite this conservation status, two popular package-holiday hotels stand within the park's limits, the Tres Islas and Oliva Beach. They pre-date the creation of the park.

Fuerteventura has another major dune area at the Istmo de la Pared, the narrow isthmus of mountainous dunes separating Jandía Peninsula from the rest of the island. At some stage in prehistory, the dunes did not exist and Jandía was a separate volcanic island.

Fuerteventura's dunes are neither barren nor lifeless. As well as forming spectacular beaches, they also support unusual plant species that can thrive in these dry, salty sands. Some are found only here, including a yellow-flowering shrub, *Lotus lancerottense*, *Echium handiense* with its bluebell flowers, and a red-flowered succulent, *Euphorbia handiensis*.

4
Fundación César Manrique

César Manrique's own home, half submerged in a string of volcanic bubbles in the rock, displays to the full his tremendous artistic flair.

Manrique had a special interest in mobiles and one extraordinary example is the huge complex of colour and movement – like an enormous children's toy – standing at the entrance to his own home. It is best seen at night, when the mobile and the house are not so much illuminated as dotted with light.

Here architecture is fun, astonishing and brilliant. The visible exterior of the building, inspired by traditional local style, combines dazzling white with jet black. Around it, a garden of cacti, succulents and semicircles of stone is set between white and black walls. Immense cylindrical cacti look like green Doric columns. Above the doorway, note Manrique's 'logo' – an interlocked C and M said to resemble a devil.

Since Manrique's death, the interior has become an art gallery, made up mainly of his private collection. It includes works by most of the big names of 20th-century abstract and modern art, including Tapies, Miró and Picasso, as well as a number of Manrique's own powerful canvases.

Steps lead down into five volcanic bubbles (created during the eruptions of 1730–36), each made into a complete room with distinctive character, colour and furniture. One has a trickling fountain, another a palm tree growing up through the roof. The dining room has an open grill, a pool filled from a black waterspout, and a dining table beneath a ceiling of rock. Narrow galleries in the rock, painted white and black to match the rest of the house, link the bubble rooms.

Every detail of Manrique's home was lovingly designed – from the foundations to the chimney top

🕂 29C2

✉ Taro de Tahíche, 5km north of Arrecife

☎ 928 84 31 38

🌐 Jul–Oct daily 10–7; Nov–Jun Mon-Sat 10–6, Sun 10–3

🍴 Snack bar (€)

🚌 No 7 (Arrecife–Máguez), No 9 (Arrecife–Orzola), several times daily each way, stop at Tahíche

ℹ Blas Cabrera Felipe (by waterfront), Arrecife ☎ 928 81 17 62

♿ Few

✋ Moderate

↔ Arrecife (► 31)

5
Islote de Hilario
(Timanfaya)

28B2

Timanfaya National
Park, 7km north of Yaiza

928 84 00 57

Daily 9–6

El Diablo (€€) restaurant
(open noon–3:30) and
snack bar (9–4:45)

None, but many coach
excursions from the
resorts

Avenida de las Playas,
Puerto del Carmen
928 51 33 51

Few

Moderate (includes
Volcano Route bus tour)

Timanfaya National Park
(► 55–61), Yaiza
(► 72), Ermita de los
Dolores (► 39)

The last Volcano Route
tour leaves at 5PM. For
car drivers, there are
extensive free parking
facilities at the Islote de
Hilario summit

*The heart and soul of Lanzarote is an awesome red
and black volcano called Islote de Hilario or Fire
Mountain, whose presence dominates the island.*

Lanzarote's Fire Mountain is still alive but taking a nap.
Every visitor to the island is drawn to its summit. Visible
from afar, the volcano dominates the view and the
thoughts of visitors and locals alike. Its catastrophic force
once destroyed in an instant the livelihood of most of the
islanders, yet it is now Lanzarote's most stunning
attraction. Of the several volcanic points in the island,
including the other mountains of fire within the national
park, this is the most terrible.

Black and red, fiery and ferocious, the swirling, sculpted
terrain all around leaves no doubt that this is truly a volcano
with a temper. Here and there tortured rocks are streaked
with colour, where stones have melted and fused in the
heat. The spectacular *malpaís* – badlands – all around the
mountain show not a blade of grass, but do support lichen
and small plants.

The usual way to climb the volcano
is to drive along a roadway that climbs
to the summit of Islote de Hilario,
where the lingering volcanic heat
remains hottest. At the very top, a big,
crowded and convivial restaurant called
El Diablo (The Devil) is an incongruous
oasis of life and enjoyment amid the
tortured, arid wilderness. Conceived
and constructed by César Manrique,
the restaurant is a glass-walled circle
giving huge, thrilling views of the
volcanic terrain and the sea beyond.
Waiters serve delicious meat, bread
and salty *papas arrugadas* and good
Lanzarote wines.

Before you go into El Diablo, take a
look at the wide opening resembling a
well, just by the entrance. This 'well'
descends into fiery earth, not water,
and the restaurant's meat and fish are
cooked in the oven-like 300°C heat that
wafts up from the volcano. At other
places close by, the surface of the
ground is too hot to walk on,
sometimes reaching 100°C. Ten
centimetres below, the temperature is
140°C; at 6m down it is 400°C; while

Opposite: *the bleak
landscape of Timanfaya
National Park*

20

the temperature just 13m underground reaches 600°C.

Outside the restaurant's panoramic glass walls, uniformed staff of the Timanfaya National Park (➤ 55–61) make the volcano do impressive tricks: a bunch of brushwood thrown into a hollow quickly bursts into flames; a bucket of water emptied into a hole roars straight back as an immense spout of steam. In front of the restaurant buses set off on the round tour of the Route of the Volcanoes, included in the park ticket price.

When Timanfaya erupted in 1730, it threw a thick layer of burning rocks over the cornfields of western Lanzarote. During the six years that the eruption continued, the fertile western end of the island was devastated, and several villages in the Timanfaya area were burned off the surface of the earth. Today life has returned to normal at villages where the lava flow stopped, like Yaiza, Uga and Mancha Blanca, and the tiny pebbles of grey-black volcanic debris – *picón* – have been found greatly to aid agriculture, and are now being sold to farmers on other Canary Islands.

Water is turned instantly to steam by the subterranean heat

6
Jameos del Agua

✝ 29D4

✉ 2km from Arrieta, 26km north of Arrecife

☎ 928 84 80 20

🕐 Daily 9:30–6:30; also Tue, Fri, Sat 7PM–1:45AM (folklore show 11PM)

🍴 Restaurant (€€, evenings only), two bars (€, all day)

🚌 No 9 (Arrecife–Orzola) several times daily each way

ℹ️ Blas Cabrera Felipe (by waterfront), Arrecife ☎ 928 81 17 62

♿ None

✋ Moderate

↔ Cueva de los Verdes (► 17)

Enjoy the experience of dining underground in this unique setting

César Manrique turned this bizarre volcanic feature into one of the island's most intriguing sights, an exotic subterranean water garden.

A *jameo* is an underground volcanic tunnel whose roof has partly collapsed. Until Manrique set to work, this one was just a hole in the ground.

Jameos del Agua is reached from the surface by spiral wooden stairs that twist down into the earth. At the bottom, astonishingly, a restaurant and dance floor look over an eerie underground lake; tiny, blind white crabs live in its perfectly transparent water. At the lake's far end, the arty tables of another bar perch on little terraces where you can sit with a meal or a drink.

This mysterious environment, within a roofless cavern below sea-level, is truly hard to comprehend at first. Whatever the weather outside, here the air is still and balmy, and full of the songs of tiny birds.

From the bar, meandering paths lead upwards among rocks and plant beds to a dazzling man-made blue and white pool. More spiral steps wind steeply up to the edges of the *jameos*, giving thrilling views down into this extraordinary meeting point of man and nature.

At the top, the Casa de los Volcanes (House of Volcanoes) is a science museum that is devoted mainly to volcanic activity.

On Tuesday, Friday and Saturday evenings, Jameos del Agua becomes a spectacular subterranean nightclub.

7

Jardín de Cactus
(Cactus Garden)

*Manrique transformed a disused quarry into this
extraordinary formal garden with over 1,400
varieties of cactus.*

The fields of cactus around Guatiza and Mala, north of
Arrecife, used to be cultivated as homes to a cochineal
beetle, whose larva provides a bright red dye. Now the
most striking landmark in the cactus district is César
Manrique's towering 8m green metal cactus outside the
entrance to his Cactus Garden.

Formerly a hand-dug quarry from which local farmers
extracted volcanic rock, the garden is an oval-shaped
enclosure descending in narrow concentric stone terraces.
Each terrace is now covered with *picón*. Growing from the
black ash like bizarre artworks are 1,420 species of cactus,
a total of almost 10,000 plants, each standing separate
from the rest and demanding attention.

Some are like porcupines, some like wedding cakes
covered in hair, some like prickly rockets, some spreading
themselves like octopuses, others uncoiling like snakes.
Some resemble rolls of barbed
wire. Others seem to have
come straight out of a Wild
West cartoon strip. Many have
florid, gaudy blooms, others
tiny, delicate flowers, sometimes strung around the plant
like a necklace.

Visitors walk carefully around
the terraces, gradually descending to a lower central area,
where there is a miniature
water garden and remnants of
the quarry. A terrace rather
wider than the rest accommo-
dates a stylish bar, where
circular wooden tables under
pale sailcloth awnings offer a
view of the entire garden.

Behind the bar, an old
windmill rises above the garden
and the surrounding landscape.
Beautifully restored, it is still
used for grinding grain.

*A restored windmill rises
behind the perfectly
arranged cacti*

✚ 29D3

✉ Guatiza (17km northeast
of Arrecife)

☎ 928 52 93 97

🕐 Daily 10–5:45

🍴 Bar/restaurant (€)
10–5:45PM

🚌 No 7 (Arrecife–Teguise)

ℹ Blas Cabrera Felipe (by
waterfront), Arrecife
☎ 928 81 17 62

♿ Few

✋ Inexpensive; admission
includes a free drink

↔ Teguise (➤ 25)

8
Mirador del Río

29D4

7km north of Haría

928 52 65 48

Daily 10–5:45

Snack bar (€)

None

To visit La Graciosa, catch a ferry from nearby Orzola

Blas Cabrera Felipe (by waterfront), Arrecife
928 81 17 62

None

Inexpensive

Haría (➤ 42)

A touch of Manrique magic has made a clifftop view of little Isla Graciosa into one of the loveliest places on the island.

A *mirador* is a viewpoint, and El Río, literally 'the river', is the name of the narrow strait between Lanzarote and its little sister island, Isla Graciosa. Outside the Mirador, one of Manrique's open metalwork signs stands in front of a daunting stone wall that actually conceals the view, with just a porthole hinting at what lies on the other side.

Before César Manrique set to work Bateria del Río, an old artillery post, perched here, 479m high on the Famara cliffs with a commanding view over La Graciosa and the islands of Montaña Clara and Alegranza beyond.

Manrique's first thought was to create a restaurant here. He had a large room chipped out of the cliff top, and roofed it with two domes covered with earth and grass. It is entered through a long, winding white tunnel and spiral staircase, which plays with brilliant effect on the themes of light, space and air.

The white room – or rooms, for the domes break up the space – is exquisite, its simplicity, clarity and spaciousness a delight to the eye. Neat wooden tables provide a place to sit and relax, and a most unusual-looking bar serves drinks and snacks. There is also a balcony, where you can stand in the open air by a sheer drop.

The main attraction, however, is the view itself, a spectacular vista of sea and sky, in which La Graciosa floats as if itself suspended like a sculpture.

Taking in the view across El Río

9
Teguise

Lanzarote's former capital is today barely more than a village, but it still has the island's most elegant buildings and greatest charm.

Until 1852 this tiny town was Lanzarote's capital, in the centre of the island, out of reach of the coast's raiders and pirates. Founded in the 15th century by Maciot de Béthencourt, nephew of Lanzarote's Norman conqueror Jean de Béthencourt, it stands on the native islanders' ancient meeting point, known as Acatife. Locals still regard this as the island's real capital, while Arrecife remains *el puerto,* the port.

Though small, Teguise has an airy, confident Iberian colonial style with a handsome square, a grid of narrow cobbled streets and a church. For a hundred years it remained the Canaries' most important town, home of European nobility – the de Béthencourts, the Herreras and others – and gave birth to much Canarian folk culture, including its unique instrument, the *timple.*

In the white lanes and pleasant plazas of Teguise today, many buildings still possess a certain splendour. In the main square is the ancient, white-capped landmark church, Iglesia de Nuestra Señora de Guadalupe (also known as San Miguel), and the impressive Renaissance mansion Palacio de Spinola (or Espíñola), former home of a wealthy 18th-century Genoese merchant, now a museum. The savings bank Caja de Canarios occupies a 15th-century tithe barn.

In the charming, smaller Plaza del 18 de Julio, the old hospital dates from 1473, and the snow-white, balconied Casa Cuartel, once an army barracks, from the 17th century. The two conventual churches, the Franciscans' 16th-century San Francisco and Dominicans' 17th-century San Domingo, are a short walk away.

Thousands of people arrive every Sunday for the morning market (► 106), one of the Canaries' largest.

Above: *the Church of Our Lady of Guadalupe*

29C3

9km north of Arrecife

Ikarus (€€), Plaza del 18 de Julio

No 6 (Arrecife–Playa Blanca) one bus each way Sun only. No 7, six times a day Mon–Fri, three to four times Sat–Sun. No 9 (Arrecife–Orzola) several times daily. Nos 11 and 12 run twice a day each way on Sun only from Costa Teguise and Puerto del Carmen respectively. Most tour operators run weekly coach trips to Teguise market on Sunday morning

San Bartolomé: Dr Cerdeña Bethancourt 17 ☎ 928 52 23 51

Castillo de Santa Bárbara (► 37)

10
Valle de la Geria

✝ 28B2

✉ East of Uga; along the Uga–Masdache road (LZ30)

ℹ Playa Grande, Puerto del Carmen ☎ 928 51 53 37

↔ Yaiza (➤ 72–73), Timanfaya National Park (➤ 55–61)

❓ Wine-growers' *bodegas* such as El Grifo and Bodegas Mozaga offer wine-tasting

Vines are grown in carefully sited hollows dug into the volcanic debris

The extraordinary vineyards in this blackened landscape are dramatic evidence of the interplay between nature's power and man's ingenuity.

It might seem unlikely that a blasted rocky terrain covered with grey volcanic debris would be among the most intriguing and even beautiful of landscapes. At first sight, the land appears hostile, barren and bleak. In places the ground has been shattered by volcanic activity, sliced and patterned by deep narrow fissures. Deep under the solid surface, molten lava is still moving.

However, look carefully. Tiny white and coloured living specks dot the dark volcanic stones – miniscule lichens and tiny succulents. Unexpected dips and hollows harbour little clusters of lush natural greenery. In spring the roadsides are lined with wild flowers, some strikingly coloured, like the purple poppies.

Most remarkable are the vineyards, each vine growing deep in a separate hollow dug into the shingly rock. Each hollow shelters behind its own semicircular rock wall. This gives the vines just enough shade and shelter to survive, and catch what little moisture can be gathered through dew and condensation. So successful is the method, in fact, that each produces some 200kg of grapes in a season. Though cleverly functional, the rows of little horseshoe walls look more like art than agriculture: César Manrique's 'landscape as art' has here become 'farming as geometry'. The vines produce Malvasia grapes, and the wine they make – fresh, dry whites with a rich, pleasant flavour – can be tasted and bought at the various *bodegas* (wine cellars) off the Uga–Masdache road and in Uga.

When stopping to explore, remember that the cutting edges of the rough, sharp, brittle black rocks and stones make walking difficult and unpleasant, and can destroy a pair of shoes in minutes.

What to See

Above: *boats in Arrecife Harbour*
Right: *harvesting onions near Teguise*

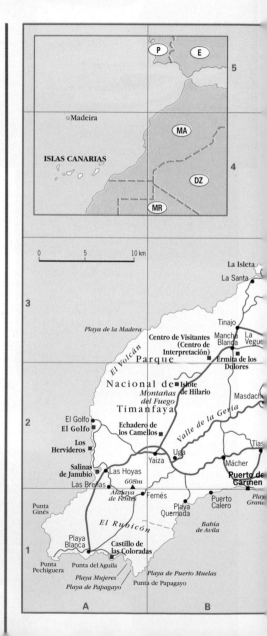

P E

5

ISLAS CANARIAS

Madeira

MA

4

DZ

MR

0   5   10 km

La Isleta

La Santa

3

Playa de la Madera

Tinajo

Mancha   La
Blanca   Vegue

Centro de Visitantes
(Centro de
Interpretación)

Ermita de los
Dolores

El Volcán   Parque

Nacional de Islote
Montañas   de Hilario
del Fuego

Masdach

Timanfaya

Valle de la Geria

El Golfo
El Golfo

2

Echadero de
los Camellos

Los
Hervideros

Uga

Tías

Yaiza

Mácher

Salinas
de Janubio

Las Hoyas

Puerto de
Carmen

608m

Las Breñas

Atalaya
de Femés

Femés

Puerto
Calero

Playa
Grana

Punta
Ginés

Playa
Quemoda

Babía
de Avila

El Rubicón

1

Playa
Blanca

Castillo de
las Coloradas

Punta
Pechiguera

Punta del Aguila

Playa de Puerto Muelas

Playa Mujeres

Playa de Papagayo

Punta de Papagayo

A   B

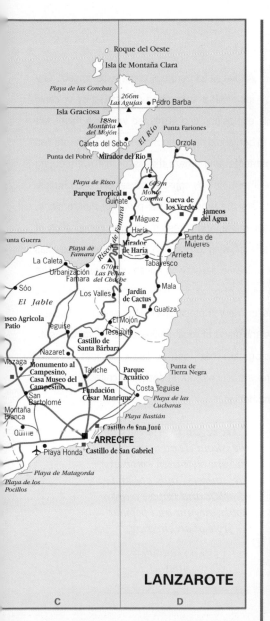

Roque del Oeste

Isla de Montaña Clara

Playa de las Conchas

266m
Las Agujas ● Pedro Barba

Isla Graciosa

188m
*Montaña
del Mojón*

Caleta del Sebo

El Río Punta Fariones

Orzola

Punta del Pobre **Mirador del Río** ■

Yé

609m
*Monte
Corona* **Cueva de
los Verdes**

Playa de Risco

Parque Tropical ■

Guinate **Jameos
del Agua**

Máguez

Haría

unta Guerra Punta de
Mujeres

*Playa de
Famara* **Mirador
de Haría**

La Caleta Arrieta

Urbanización
Famara 670m
*Las Peñas
del Chache* Tabayesco

● Sóo Mala

El Jable Los Valles **Jardín
de Cactus**

seo Agrícola
Patio El Mojón Guatiza

Teguise Tesegüite

**Castillo de
Santa Bárbara**

Nazaret

Mozaga **Monumento al
Campesino,
Casa Museo del
Campesino** Tahiche **Parque
Acuático** Punta de
Tierra Negra

San
Bartolomé **Fundación
César Manrique** Costa Teguise

Montaña
Blanca *Playa de las
Cucharas*

Güime *Playa Bastián*

Castillo de San José ■

ARRECIFE

✈ Playa Honda **Castillo de San Gabriel**

Playa de Matagorda

*Playa de los
Pocillos*

LANZAROTE

C D

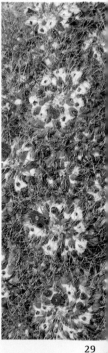

*Cactus flowers at César
Manrique's Jardín de
Cactus*

29

Lanzarote

Above all Lanzarote is about visual impact. Any idea that a little island devastated by volcanic explosions and blanketed with lava might not have much to see could hardly be more wrong. Lanzarote has so much to interest and amaze the visitor that every outing seems to be interrupted by constant pauses and photo stops. Some sights are the product of the power of nature alone, some are man-made, and some an intriguing combination of the two. It's fascinating to see how man's inventiveness has turned the volcanic activity to advantage, especially the covering of acres of good soil with *picón*, black volcanic grit that absorbs any dew or precipitation and helps crops flourish. Everywhere the hand of local genius César Manrique, self-styled 'ecological artist', can be seen, not just in major artworks and attractions, but in cottage architecture, colour schemes and design.

> *We began to give back to the island its own original, volcanic character, emphasise its unique landscape and improve and impose a clear, sober, elegant and popular style of architecture.*

CÉSAR MANRIQUE,
1981

Arrecife

Until the last century Arrecife was no more than a small working port. Inland Teguise was the island's capital and market centre, well away from the raiders who harried the coast. That's why Arrecife is still known to many locals simply as *el puerto* (the port). To protect itself, Arrecife built the two fine fortresses that still watch over its harbours today. As the coastal danger declined and trade increased, Arrecife grew, finally becoming the capital of Lanzarote in 1852.

If, while touring Lanzarote, you ever wonder 'Where is everybody?', the answer is, 'in Arrecife'. Today half the islanders live in the capital, and many more come here to work each day. A striking, in some ways rather satisfying, contrast to the picturesque strangeness of the rest of the island, Arrecife is an ordinary, hardworking Spanish town making few concessions to tourists. Having expanded well before the days of César Manrique, this is the one place on the island that really does not conform to his aesthetic guidelines. Indeed, Lanzarote's most unsightly modern buildings are here.

There are pretty places too, such as the town's excellent El Reducto main beach and its old harbour, with the waterside gardens and promenade, are a delight. The other places of interest, too, are all close to the sea, and the main tourist office is also here on Blas Cabrera Felipe. A new coastal path heading south means that you can now walk all the way to Puerto del Carmen – past the airport – without going on a road.

San Ginés Church is at the heart of Arrecife

31

What to See in Arrecife

CASTILLO DE SAN GABRIEL ✪

Poised on a tiny islet called Islote de los Ingleses, just off the main town centre old harbour, Castillo de San Gabriel adds charm to Arrecife's waterfront. Built in 1590 by Italian architect Leonardo Torriani on part of the string of rocky islets off the town, the castle became a vital part of the defences protecting the harbour and town from marauding pirates. A low, sturdy, square and rather featureless structure, the castle is made more appealing by its honey-coloured stonework and the islet setting.

One of the most endearing features of the castle today – though it once had a serious military function – is that to reach it you must walk out along a walled mole. There is now a second causeway giving access for permitted vehicles, while the original is for pedestrians only. The causeway passes over a small drawbridge, known as the Puente de las Bolas – the Bridge of the Balls – because of the two cannon balls perched on top.

🞢 34C1
✉ Avenida Gen Franco
🚌 From Avenida Gen Franco

Some weatherbeaten old cannons stand outside the castle. The view back towards the harbour and promenade puts Arrecife in a better light, with the white-capped San Ginés church belfry and the whitewashed houses of the little town standing out against the volcanic terrain beyond.

The small archaeological museum inside the castle is currently closed for renovation, a completion date is yet to be confirmed.

CASTILLO DE SAN JOSÉ (➤ 16, TOP TEN)

EL CHARCO DE SAN GINÉS
Sometimes mistakenly thought by visitors to be the name of Arrecife's old harbour, the Charco lies back from the sea within the town centre. This curious little lake or lagoon of sea water, surrounded by a walkway and modest fishermen's cottages, is said to lie at the very origin of Arrecife. The legendary San Ginés lived here as a hermit beside the water. A village of pious fishing folk grew around the hermitage, and as the village expanded into a town, the hermitage became the town's church. There are several such lagoons around the Lanzarote coastline, for example El Charco de Janubio (➤ 66) and El Charco north of Costa Teguise (➤ 38); these have been put to use as salt pans, producing a coarse salt for preserving fish.

✚	34C2
✉	Avenida Vargos
🍴	Cafés (€) on waterfront
🚌	From Avenida La Marina
♿	Few
🎟	Free

IGLESIA DE SAN GINÉS
Arrecife's main church, this dignified little building of dark volcanic stone and bright white paintwork is dedicated to the town's patron saint. It was built in the 18th century when Arrecife was no more than a harbour village. Handsomely restored, the church is still at the old heart of the town, standing at one end of a pleasant square. Restoration has given the church a facelift, and inside it has an attractive Moorish ceiling. Formerly the hermitage of Ginés, it stands beside the El Charco lagoon, and to the locals their devotion to San Ginés is part of the town's marine tradition.

✚	34C2
✉	Plaza de San Ginés
⏰	Open to public daily 9–1, 5–7 except during church services
🚌	From Avenida La Marina
♿	None
🎟	Free
❓	Annual Fiesta de San Ginés in August with processions, parades and traditional dancing inthe streets

Left: *El Charco de San Ginés is a seawater lagoon in the heart of the town*

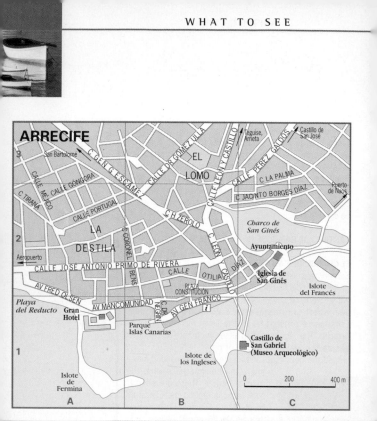

ARRECIFE

A
B
C

Around Arrecife

The relaxed little capital of Lanzarote is where the real, modern life of the island is lived. Start at the tourist information office on the waterfront, an attractive pavilion made of volcanic stone and carved timbers.

Walk north, with the sea on your right, along the promenade as far as Calle León y Castillo. Turn right into the short street Calle Ginés de Castro y Alverez.

This comes to the church dedicated to San Ginés, Arrecife's patron saint (➤ 33).

Turn right and right again and follow the whitewashed lanes to the Charco de San Ginés (➤ 33). Follow the quiet promenade that runs all the way round the Charco, including a bridge across the entrance to the lagoon.

At the inland end of the lagoon, short lanes lead back to Calle León y Castillo.

Turn left into Calle León y Castillo, towards the sea. Turn right at Calle Gen Goded and follow the direction of traffic along Calle Alferez Cabrera Tavio to Plaza de la Constitución. Cross the square to the far corner and turn left and right into Calle Luis Morote and follow this back street, with its glimpses of the sea.

On a busy corner dozens of café tables are set out beside Calle Dr Negrín. Ahead you can see the five-star Gran Hotel, Lanzarote's tallest (and ugliest) building.

Turn left along Avenida Mancomunidad. The road turns right and left to approach the promenade gardens and then to return to the tourist information pavilion.

Distance
5km

Time
2 hours

Start/end point
Tourist office
✚ 34B1

Lunch
Several bars and restaurants
(€–€€) along Calle León y Castillo

Left: *the 16th-century Castillo de San Gabriel still guards the town's waterfront*

Below: *another golden sunrise over Arrecife Harbour*

What to See around Lanzarote

28A1
Playa Blanca
Free access
Many bars and
restaurants (€–€€) in
Playa Blanca
Free
Playa Blanca (➤ 62–63),
Papagayo (➤ 50–51)

ÁGUILA ✪

Standing on a promontory called Punta del Águila (Eagle Point), between the beautiful Playa Blanca and Playa Papagayo beaches on the island's southern shore, the restored circular watchtower called Castillo de las Coloradas (or Torre del Águila – Aguila Tower) stands guard beside the beach where de Béthencourt is said to have made his first landing on Lanzarote in 1402. However, he had already dropped anchor in El Río and stepped on to the island of Graciosa. Another local story is that de Béthencourt himself erected the tower, though in fact it was built much later; it bears the date of 1769, and it is thought most of the present structure is even older, dating from 1778. There are good views from here across the straits to Fuerteventura.

29D3
22km north of Arrecife
Good fish restaurants (€)
facing the jetty
Four times daily from
Arrecife
Few
Cueva de los Verdes
(➤ 17), Jameos del Agua
(➤ 22)

ARRIETA ✪

Arrieta is a relatively undeveloped, traditional small town of simple low white houses on the island's northeast coast; it is little known to visitors but nevertheless makes an interesting pause after a trip to the nearby Jameos del Agua (➤ 22) or Cueva de los Verdes (➤ 17). Its attractions include one of several fine beaches to be found along this part of the coast, and a picturesque harbour with a quay made of volcanic rock.

Did you know ?

Why did de Béthencourt settle around Águila instead of El Río and Famara, where he had first arrived? For sailing ships, the trade winds were a danger on the north and west, while this southern coast is the island's most sheltered. Secondly, the flat southern plain gave much easier access to the interior.

CASTILLO DE SANTA BÁRBARA (OR GUANAPAY) AND MUSEO DEL EMIGRANTE CANARIO ✪

A fine castle standing proudly on the summit of volcanic Mount Guanapay, overlooking the little town of Teguise, the Castillo de Santa Bárbara was for centuries a vital defence against Moorish raiders, who came inland as far as the island's old capital. The fortress was first erected in the 14th century by Lancelotto Malocello, the voyager who gave his name to the island, reconstructed 100 years later by Maciot de Béthencourt, and further strengthened in the 16th century.

Distinctive for its pale golden stone on an island where almost everything is either black or white, the castle dominates the area of villa developments around Oasis de Nazaret. The views alone amply reward a visit.

Inside the castle today an Emigrant Museum tells the stirring, sometimes tragic, story of how the poorest Canary Islanders have left in search of a better life. During certain periods in the past, the people of Lanzarote emigrated en masse to South America. Among other things, we learn that natives of different Canary Islands settled in different countries. Lanzaroteños mainly went to Venezuela, while people from Fuerteventura emigrated to Cuba.

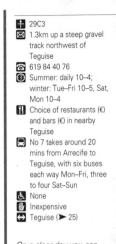

✚ 29C3

✉ 1.3km up a steep gravel track northwest of Teguise

☎ 619 84 40 76

🕐 Summer: daily 10–4; winter: Tue–Fri 10–5, Sat, Mon 10–4

🍴 Choice of restaurants (€) and bars (€) in nearby Teguise

🚌 No 7 takes around 20 mins from Arrecife to Teguise, with six buses each way Mon–Fri, three to four Sat–Sun

♿ None

💷 Inexpensive

↔ Teguise (► 25)

On a clear day you can see for miles from the splendidly sited Santa Bárbara Castle

➕ 29D2

✉ On the coast 7km
northwest of Arrecife

🍴 Beachside
bar–restaurants (€€)

🚌 No 1 from Arrecife every
20 minutes throughout
the day Mon–Fri, every
30 minutes at weekends
and festivals. Journey
takes 20 minutes

♿ Good

🔁 Arrecife (➤ 31–35),
Fundación César
Manrique (➤ 19)

*Playa de las Cucharas,
Costa Teguise's open,
windswept main beach*

COSTA TEGUISE ✪✪

Some maps of the island on sale in local shops still do not
show Costa Teguise. Within a few years this carefully
planned, purpose-built resort town has sprung up
alongside excellent beaches 5km up the coast from
Arrecife. The quality of the accommodation and facilities is
above the average for the Canaries, and represents good
value for money, so Costa Teguise now attracts large
numbers of holiday visitors, many of them self-catering.

Costa Teguise has also proved attractive to well-to-do
Spanish celebrities, a number of whom have holiday
homes here. But the resort feels unfocused and has an
unfinished look in parts. It is a narrow ribbon development
with three different focal points (Bastian, Jablillo and
Cucharas). Obviously there is no 'old quarter', and a string
of *centros comerciales* (shopping centres) and holiday
apartment blocks backs onto the beach. Although everything is low-rise and has broadly been guided by the
principles laid down by César Manrique, the new buildings
are modern and sometimes charmless.

Yet what the resort lacks in history or character is made
up for by a location ideal for sun, sea, sand, sport and
sightseeing. In addition to the main, long, sandy Las
Cucharas beach there are other waterfront areas, including
a sandy beach at Jablillo. Watersports facilities and rentals
are available, and there is also an aquapark. An 18-hole golf
course is on the northern edge of town.

CUEVA DE LOS VERDES (► 17, TOP TEN)

ERMITA DE LOS DOLORES (HERMITAGE OF THE SORROWS) ✪

Pilgrims flock to this beautiful church in the village of Mancha Blanca, especially on 15 September, the feast day of the Virgin of the Volcanoes. The village stands above the desolate *malpaís* at the point where it meets neatly farmed, highly productive fields layered with *picón*.

The Hermitage of the Sorrows – a gracious building with a cupola and a plain white interior – was built in honour of the Virgin of the Volcanoes, patron saint of Lanzarote, after she saved the village from destruction. It happened during the island's most recent volcanic eruption, in 1824, when lava and fire poured down from the Tinguatón volcano. The blazing liquid crept its way towards the village, igniting all in its path. Local people prayed fervently, begging Our Lady to spare them. The pious can prove that she listened to their pleas, for the lava flow did come to a halt – stopped, they say, by the Virgin's veil – at the very foot of Mancha Blanca village. The exact spot where the Virgin must have stood has been marked by a cross, placed at the edge of the *malpaís*.

In contrast to the miraculous intervention in the volcanic eruptions, Mancha Blanca also has an important National Park Interpretation Centre with a permanent exhibition on the vulcanology of the Canary Islands, and Lanzarote in particular (► 58).

The Virgin of the Volcanoes in her church at Mancha Blanca

- 🔲 28B3
- ⊠ Mancha Blanca
- 🕐 Open all day every day; locked at night
- 🍴 Bar–restaurant (€€) across the road
- 💵 Donations welcome
- ↔ Islote de Hilario (► 20–21), Timanfaya National Park (► 55–61)
- ❓ Processions and celebrations on the Fiesta de la Virgen de los Volcanes, every year on 15 Sep

Above: *playing on the vast sandy beach at Famara*

FAMARA ⭐⭐

Most tourist development has been on the sheltered southern and eastern coasts of the island, but the north coast has some glorious golden sandy beaches too. One of the very best is Playa de Famara – so good that visitors are prepared to put up with the slightly more temperamental weather and that little bit of extra wind that comes from the northwest. The ocean currents are also more dangerous here, so swimming and diving are discouraged, although windsurfers are drawn to this beach.

At one end of the beach, La Caleta de Famara – a small, working fishing village and low-key resort – makes for an enjoyable stroll, or even a good place to stay on this side of the island. It is particularly popular with anglers.

Rising behind the shore towards the other end of the beach, the spectacular Riscos de Famara (Famara Cliffs) reach a height of almost 450m. These cliffs, with their exquisite sea views out towards Graciosa Island (► 43), continue – under different names – as far as the Mirador del Río (► 24) and beyond.

FEMÉS ⭐

This likeable, secluded little village on the back road to Playa Blanca is perched on a rocky ledge surrounded by hills, with good views across the Rubicón plain to the south. Serious walkers can enjoy an even better panorama by climbing the Atalaya de Femés, a 608m volcanic peak with breathtaking views to Timanfaya in one direction and Fuerteventura in the other. Femés was one of the first European settlements on the island, and the village church of San Marcial de Rubicón was the first cathedral to be built in the Canary Islands.

FUNDACIÓN CÉSAR MANRIQUE (► 19, TOP TEN)

 29C3
⊠ 11km north of Teguise
🍴 Several simple restaurants (€)
🚌 No 18 runs four times a day, between La Caleta and Arrecife
↔ Haría (► 42), Mirador del Río (► 24)

➕ 28A1
⊠ 5km south of Uga; 8km north of Playa Blanca
🍴 Several restaurants (€–€€) in Playa Blanca
🚌 No 5 between Femés and Arrecife two or three times a day Mon–Fri
↔ Playa Blanca (► 62), Águila (► 36), Papagayo (► 50), Uga (► 72)

EL GOLFO (THE GOLF) ★

On the southwestern shore of the island, El Golfo is the extraordinary result of a meeting between the blackened volcanic devastation of Timanfaya and the power of the Atlantic waves. Here the half-submerged cone of a volcano has been eroded and transformed into a bizarre natural attraction. Over time, the ocean has eaten into the volcanic crater, leaving a lagoon surrounded by an amphitheatre of lava cliff, the rock streaked and stained with a multitude of strange reds and russets.

Most remarkable is the colour of the lagoon. A number of factors, including volcanic minerals and algae, have given the water a deep, intense emerald hue, especially brilliant when it catches the sun, and a very striking contrast to the glorious blue sea that lies beside it.

Although linked to the ocean, the lagoon appears quite separate from it – the connection is through volcanic passages hidden underground.

To reach the lagoon, follow the access road on the left 2km before the village of El Golfo. On reaching the car park continue on foot, following signs for a short walk around the headland.

Between El Golfo village and the lagoon there are a number of sheltered bays with black beaches. The seashore village of El Golfo itself has rather an end-of-the-road feel, but has become a centre for enticing fish restaurants.

The green water of the lagoon contrasts sharply with the striated sandstone cliffs of the extinct volcano

➕ 28A2
✉ 12km northwest of Yaiza
🍴 About a dozen small restaurants (€) in El Golfo village serve fresh fish and shellfish
✋ Free
↔ Los Hervideros (➤ 43), Salinas de Janubio (➤ 66), Timanfaya (➤ 55), Yaiza (➤ 72)

🔳 29D3

✉ 15km north of Teguise

🍴 Snack bars (€) on the southern edge of town; Restaurante El Cortijo (€€) serves classic Lanzarote dishes

🚌 No 7 from Arrecife; the journey takes about 1 hour

↔ Arrieta (➤ 36), Mirador del Río (➤ 24)

❓ Fiesta de San Juan celebrates midsummer on 24 Jun. It is preceeded by 2 or 3 days of events

Palm trees thrive in Haría village

HARÍA ⭐⭐

In contrast to Lanzarote's clichéd image as a volcanic island with a lunar landscape, here in the north of the island is a delightful little hill town in a lush green valley. Surprisingly, it is perfectly tranquil and unspoiled, with few visitors. The narrow streets and lanes are speckled with colour where purple bougainvillaea and red pelargoniums climb brilliant white walls. Stroll past some fine houses and pretty corners to reach a main square shaded by a canopy of leafy branches and loud with sparrows.

The setting of the village is especially striking, among a cool, green patchwork of fields and wildflower meadows shaded by palm trees. Poetically, this has been dubbed the Valley of 1,000 Palms – or even, sometimes, the Valley of 10,000 Palms! Some dispute the locals' claim that they have more palm trees here than anywhere else in the Canaries, but many plant species do grow in this valley that botanists have not found on any other Canary island. You will also see several types of cactus.

One of the best places to get an overview of this haven is from the Mirador de Haría, a high viewpoint beside the twisting main road as it hairpins round the heights of the Galería de Famara 5km south of Haría.

LOS HERVIDEROS ✪

On the western shore, where the dark volcanic *malpaís* descends into the blue Atlantic waves, a *mirador* (viewpoint) looks across at a place where the ocean thunders in and out of sea caverns. The turbulent, bubbling effect has been called Los Hervideros, the boiling waters.

> ### *Did you know ?*
>
> *The names of Lanzarote's offshore islands suggest how they were seen by sailors after the two-day journey from Spain. Their first sight of land would have been the larger isles which were named Grace (Graciosa), Clear Mountain (Montaña Clara) and Joy (Alegranza). However, the dangerous smaller islet they called Hell Rock (Roque del Inferno).*

- ✚ 28A2
- ✉ 3km off Yaiza–Playa Blanca road
- 🍴 Nearby restaurants (€) in El Golfo, Janubio or Yaiza
- ↔ El Golfo (► 41), Salinas de Janubio (► 66), Yaiza (► 73), Timanfaya National Park (► 55–61)

ISLA GRACIOSA ✪✪

La Graciosa is the island that rests at the centre of the view from the Mirador del Río (► 24). For many who come to admire it, this is as near as they get to the island. However, La Graciosa is easily reached and a trip there makes an enjoyable day out.

Administratively, La Graciosa is part of Lanzarote. The channel (El Río) between the two islands is just 2km wide, though the ferry goes the long way round and takes 20 minutes. With a total area of only 41sq km, the island is small enough for keen walkers to circumnavigate in a day; it receives few visitors and is a haven of tranquillity.

Yet La Graciosa is not quite as deserted as might be thought. It has two sleepy fishing villages, Caleta del Sebo (literally 'Greasy Cove', named after the whale blubber found on the beach) and Pedro Barba, both on the channel between the two islands, as well as superb golden sandy beaches and a couple of simple bar-restaurants and basic *pensiones*. And the view from La Graciosa towards the Riscos de Famara and Mirador del Río is almost as good as the view from Lanzarote. Perhaps the island's most enjoyable feature is the lack of cars – no motor vehicles are allowed. There aren't even any roads.

Away from the shore, La Graciosa consists of dunes and treeless volcanic terrain. Despite this, it was at La Graciosa that Norman conqueror Jean de Béthencourt first stepped ashore after his journey from Europe.

- ✚ 29C4
- ✉ 2km off northern shore of Lanzarote
- 🍴 Two basic bar-restaurants (€) at Caleta del Sebo, near the ferry terminal
- 🚌 No 9 bus leaves Arrecife at 7:40AM to reach Orzola in time for the 10AM ferry to La Graciosa. Return to Arrecife on the 4:30PM bus from Orzola.
- ⛴ The daily morning ferry departs Orzola at 10AM, midday and 5PM and treturns from La Caleta del Sebo at 8AM, 11AM and 4PM. Don't miss the last boat – unless you want to spend the night on the island
- ♿ None
- ↔ Orzola (► 48), Mirador del Río (► 24)

Exploring La Graciosa

Distance
18km

Time
4 hours

Start point
Caleta del Sebo
 29D4
From Orzola at 10AM
To Orzola leaves Arrecife at 7:40AM

End point
La Caleta del Sebo
29D4
Back to Orzola at 4PM
Bus to Arrecife leaves Orzola when ferry passengers have disembarked, at 4:30PM

Lunch
Bars (€)
 Caleta del Sebo

Take the 10AM ferry from Lanzarote to La Graciosa, which takes 20 minutes to reach La Graciosa's tiny port of Caleta del Sebo. The walk takes in Las Agujas (The Needles) and the Pedro Barba ridge, which form a mountain at the centre of the island.

Walk along the village quayside, then turn right (at the bar) on a footpath and then take the dirt road towards the Pedro Barba ridge.

La Graciosa's two volcanoes stand either side of the track: Mojón to the left and Pedro Barba to the right. The third peak which comes into view between them is Montaña Clara, a separate island. Behind is a fine view of the village and Riscos de Famara.

At a fork keep right, and head towards the holiday homes at Pedro Barba.

You are walking around the foot of Pedro Barba volcano. The rocky island of Alegranza comes into view.

Where the track forks again continue on the left. The right-hand path heads down to Pedro Barba village, which makes an agreeable diversion.

The track skirts the northern slopes of Pedro Barba, with dunes away to the right, and a sea view of Alegranza. Ahead rises Montaña Bermeja, and the cone of Pedro Barba comes into view again.

La Graciosa seen from Mirador del Río

As the track heads away from Pedro Barba and towards the foot of Montaña Bermeja, take a turn on the left which leads you back in the direction of Lanzarote.

On the right is a spectacular beach of black rock and golden sand, called Playa de las Conchas. Ahead is the dramatic coast of Lanzarote.

A left turn takes the track south, again with Mojón on one side of the path (this time on the right) and Pedro Barba on the other. When the Riscos de Famara come into view, it's not much further to Caleta del Sebo.

ISLOTE DE HILARIO (➤ 20–21, TOP TEN)

JAMEOS DEL AGUA (➤ 22, TOP TEN)

JARDÍN DE CACTUS (➤ 23, TOP TEN)

MIRADOR DEL RÍO (➤ 24, TOP TEN)

MONUMENTO AL CAMPESINO AND CASA-MUSEO DEL CAMPESINO (MONUMENT/MUSEUM HOUSE OF THE FARMER) ✪✪✪

The *campesino* is the countryman, the peasant farmer and man of the soil, whom César Manrique considered to be the very backbone of every nation, and the foundation on which its history and culture stands.

The white Campesino Monument is Manrique's tribute to the hard-working farming people of Lanzarote, who have long battled with the inhospitable terrain of their native island. Deeply moved by the labours that created the vineyards of La Geria (➤ 26), he named the 15m-high work *El Monumento Fecundidad al Campesino Lanzaroteño* (*The Fertility Monument to the Lanzarote Peasant*). Manrique dedicated the sculpture, which stands prominently at a road junction outside the wine village of Mozaga, 'to the forgotten endeavours of the unknown farmers of Lanzarote'.

The enigmatic cubist monument was constructed in 1968 from farm debris, water tanks and old fishing boats.

The Casa-Museo del Campesino is a copy of a fine traditional farm building and farmyard presented as a pristine black, white and green artwork. You can see an old preserved kitchen, tools and equipment, as well as a reproduction of a cottage workshop. In keeping with Manrique's ideas, an attractive farm-style restaurant at the site serves Lanzarote dishes.

A traditional water-purifier displayed at the Campesino Museum

➕ 29C2
✉ Between San Bartolomé and Mozaga
☎ 928 52 01 36
🕐 Daily 10–5:45
🍴 Restaurant (€)
🕐 1–4
🚌 Nos 16 and 20 to Tinajo, La Santa and Sóo
♿ Few
💷 Free
↔ La Geria (➤ 26), Teguise (➤ 25), San Bartolomé (➤ 66)

Northern Lanzarote

Distance
66km

Time
5 hours

Start/end point
Arrecife
✚ 29C2

Lunch
Restaurants in Haría (€€), and
at the Mirador del Río (€)

This trip around the northeastern half of the island heads towards a Lanzarote that is awesome and yet pretty. Avoid this drive on Sunday, as the Teguise market brings thousands of people onto this route.

From Arrecife take the main road to Teguise. Note the Manrique mobile sculptures at the junction before Tahíche. César Manrique's extraordinary home is nearby (➤ 19).

Except for a strip of *malpaís* to the left of the road, most visible at Tahíche, the countryside is rolling hills of grass and, in spring, abundant wild flowers. As you approach Teguise, the hill of Guanapay, topped by Santa Bárbara Castle (➤ 37) comes into view. Teguise (➤ 25) deserves a leisurely visit on foot.

Follow the road to Haría, which soon begins to really climb and wind before descending to the town.

On the high plateaux and peaks there are windmills – not the picturesque and old-fashioned kind, but modern wind generators. The high, winding road is airy and enjoyable to drive along, with many outstanding views. In particular, beside a bar-restaurant at a mountain pass, is the beautiful viewpoint called Mirador de Haría (➤ 42). The descent into the green valley of Haría, dotted with palms, is delightful.

Now straighter, the road continues to Yé. Turn left here to Mirador del Río.

A lovely view of Haría from a mirador on the road

The Mirador del Río (► 24) deserves a stop. A narrow road to the left of the viewpoint is now closed to vehicles and makes a thrilling clifftop stroll.

Turn south again, at first on the same road; after 2km take a left fork and wind sharply downhill towards the coast.

Enjoying the sun and the view at Mirador del Río

Jameos del Agua (► 22) and Cueva de los Verdes (► 17) are nearby and well worth a visit.

Turn right onto the coast road, which skirts Arrieta (► 36), crosses the cactus fields and passes in front of the entrance of the Jardín de Cactus (► 23). At Tahíche, turn left to return to Arrecife.

*Visit El Patio Agricultural
Museum's perfectly
restored windmill
(opposite); all the
components, including
the wooden gears (right)
have been lovingly crafted
from traditional materials*

MUSEO AGRÍCOLA EL PATIO ⊙⊙⊙
(EL PATIO AGRICULTURAL MUSEUM)

In a suitably rural location at the centre of the island, this
agricultural museum has exhibits on life in the countryside
around 50 to 100 years ago and gives an opportunity to
see and learn about Lanzarote's intriguing, ingenious and
unusual farming traditions. More than a museum, this is a
peaceful, immaculately restored traditional farm, where
visitors are guided round to take a close look inside one of
the restored windmills and farm buildings, see a garden of
cacti and other island plants, and contemplate the displays
of farm tools, local architecture, ancient ceramics, and
photographs of Lanzarote's traditional hard-working rustic
lifestyle. At the end of the tour you may taste wines
produced on the estate.

ORZOLA ⊙

Close to the northern tip of Lanzarote, on the edge of the
malpaís formed by La Corona volcano, this little working
fishing harbour is the terminal for a ferry that crosses three
times a day to Isla Graciosa, the small island that faces El
Mirador del Río (➤ 24). Orzola makes a good base for
keen anglers, while for those who would rather eat a fish
than catch one, it's also an excellent lunch stop. There are
good beaches nearby, too.

Did you know ?

*The islanders developed an ingenious way of
fishing without line, rod or net. The juice of the
candelabra cactus was squeezed out of the plant
and emptied into tidal pools when they were full
of fish. Alive, but stunned by the juice, the fish
became motionless, ready for collection.*

PAPAGAYO ✪✪

Breezy Punta de Papagayo (Papagayo Point) and the more sheltered sandy bays either side of it lie at Lanzarote's southernmost tip. These are just about the finest beaches on the island: sweeps of fine golden sand edged by the clear waters of the channel separating Lanzarote from Fuerteventura. Oddly, these excellent beaches can prove hard to find, and some still have to be reached on unmade roads with few, if any, signposts to guide the driver. Despite this, they do attract plenty of visitors, and they can get almost crowded at times.

The main beach, Playa de Papagayo (*papagayo* means parrot), is barely more than 15 minutes' drive from the resort town of Playa Blanca. As the most easily accessible beach from Playa Blanca (just continue a little way past Águila), it is also the most popular.

The ruined hamlet of El Papagayo, which is also sign-posted, is now home to sun-loving hippies. A string of other lovely beaches stretching around the peninsula of Punta de Papagayo, backed by sandy cliffs, are best reached on foot: Playa de los Pozos, Playa de Mujeres, and beyond the point, the nudists' secluded favourite, Playa de Puerto Muelas or La Caleta del Congrio. Be warned, however: none of these beaches has any shade, so you will have to carry your own.

All along this sandy stretch of coast, there are superb views to Fuerteventura – and from high points on the cliffs you can even see Puerto del Carmen and Arrecife. It seems certain that as time passes this part of Lanzarote will become a major tourist centre. For the moment though, it remains fairly unspoiled and is strictly for beach connoisseurs and sun-seekers.

The secluded beaches of Papagayo are perfect for determined sun-lovers

Volcanoes

All the Canary Islands are volcanoes and were formed by volcanic eruptions, though at very different times. The oldest of the islands is Fuerteventura, which emerged from the sea with tremendous force some 20 million years ago. It was a full four million years later that the next major volcanic eruption brought forth another island from the sea, Lanzarote.

These two were the only islands for another two or three million years. Gradually, the other islands were born, each with its own volcanic core.

Today the Canaries remain volcanic. Mount Teide on Tenerife was actually erupting as Christopher Columbus sailed by on his way to discover the Americas in 1492, and has had renewed outbursts of activity approximately every hundred years since – there could be another eruption at any time now. The most recent eruption was on La Palma in 1971, but it was relatively mild. While some island volcanoes are merely dozing, like Tenerife and Lanzarote, others have shown no sign of life for millenia, like Fuerteventura, whose volcanic terrain has broken down, and, to a large extent, been covered by wind-borne sand from the Sahara.

'Rope' lava being colonised by lichen and succulents

Lanzarote is the Canary island that is the most physically and culturally dominated by its still-smouldering volcanic power. The eruption of Timanfaya and the other Mountains of Fire between 1730 and 1736 constituted one of the longest and most powerful periods of volcanic activity ever known. It totally devastated the southern third of the island, creating a blackened, lifeless *malpaís* of cinders, ash and lava. This was enlarged by another lengthy eruption from 1812 to 1824. Both eruptions considerably increased the overall surface area of the island.

The landscapes of Lanzarote and Fuerteventura clearly demonstrate the usual volcanic process of a single major cone creating a number of smaller cones all around as outlets for gases and liquids. Lanzarote also has many examples of underground tunnels formed by gas blowing through molten rock, some of which have collapsed; for good examples of these, visit the Cueva de los Verdes (► 17) and Jameos del Agua (► 22).

The Lanzarote *malpaís*, both inside and outside the limits of the Timanfaya National Park, has good examples of all the various kinds of volcanic material thrown forth by volcanoes: pyroclasts (ash and dust particles); *picón* or lapilli (small solid particles); escoria, scoriae or pumice (lightweight fragments of rock shot through with air bubbles); bombs (large pieces of solid rock scattered about) and – most familiar of all – lava (liquid rock that flows along the ground and then slowly sets solid in ropey formations). Much has been discovered, too, about the way in which volcanic terrain is gradually colonised by flora and fauna from observing the encroachment of tiny lichens onto Lanzarote's volcanic surface.

Two outstanding places to learn more about volcanoes are open to the public on Lanzarote: the Mancha Blanca Visitor and Interpretation Centre (► 58), on the edge of the Timanfaya National Park, and the Casa de los Volcanes, or House of Volcanoes, at the Jameos del Agua grotto (► 22). Both have a wealth of displays, diagrams and models explaining how volcanoes work and how they created the Canary Islands.

Escaping gases cause openings like this hornito *in Timanfaya National Park*

How Volcanoes Work

Inside the earth, rock is a boiling liquid called magma. Where the surface crust is weak or broken, magma sometimes forces its way out through long hollows called pipes. Bursting out as solids, liquids and gases, it builds deposits into a volcanic cone. Eruptions can break out of a volcano's sides or blow gases through underground tunnels.

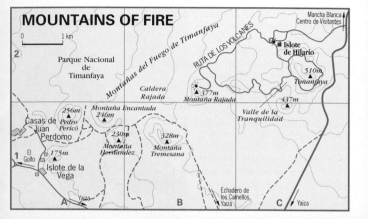

MOUNTAINS OF FIRE

0   1 km

2

Parque Nacional
de
Timanfaya

Montañas del Fuego de Timanfaya

RUTA DE LOS VOLCANES

Mancha Blanca
Centro de Visitantes

▪ Islote
de Hilario

510m
▲ *Timanfaya*

Caldera
Rajada

▲ 377m
Montaña Rajada

▲ 437m

▲ 256m
*Pedro
Pericó*

▲ Montaña Encantada
246m

Valle de la
Tranquilidad

Casas de
Juan
Perdomo

▲ 230m
*Montaña
Hernández*

▲ 328m
*Montaña
Tremesana*

1

El
Golfo

□ ▲ 175m

□ Islote de la
Vega

Echadero de
los Camellos,
Yaiza

↙ Yaiza

A

B

C

↓ Yaiza

Parque Nacional de Timanfaya (Timanfaya National Park)

Unlike most of the world's national parks, at first sight this one has no animal life, no birdlife, and not a blade of grass, flower or shrub growing anywhere. Instead the eye must become accustomed to a vast landscape of twisted and convoluted devastation. A stylised devil is the symbol of the park. With his horns, tail and trident, he conjures up a sense of mischief and fun, but while the Mountains of Fire may be fun to visit, they are a serious power. There are 36 volcanic cones within the park's 8sq km, and though they are peaceful enough at the moment, these volcanoes are still active. The black and grey desert of clinker and ash that surrounds the cones is the result of 26 eruptions between 1730 and 1736.

The start of those events was witnessed by a local man, the priest of Yaiza, Don Andrés Lorenzo Curbelo, who described them in his diary: 'On the first day of September 1730, between nine and ten at night, the earth suddenly opened close to Timanfaya, two leagues from Yaiza. During the first night an enormous mountain rose up from the bowels of the earth, with flames shooting from its summit, which continued burning for 19 days.'

A later entry in the diary recorded: 'On 18 October three new openings formed above Santa Catalina from which dense smoke emerged, which scattered over the entire island. The explosions which accompanied this phenomena, the darkness caused by the mass of grains and the smoke which covered the island, forced the inhabitants of Yaiza to flee their homes'.

Yaiza was lucky. Eleven other farming villages and hamlets were totally destroyed. Seventy years later, a series of earthquakes rocked the area again, culminating in the eruption of El Tinguatón volcano in 1824. The extraordinary terrain of Timanfaya was finally declared a national park in 1974.

Left: *view from Yaiza, on the edge of the park*
Below: *camels take tourists up the steep side of Timanfaya Mountain*

The Tremesana Route

Reservations
You need to book in advance to join this guided walk (☎ 928 84 08 39). It can be done on Monday, Wednesday and Friday.

Distance
3km

Time
3 hours

Start/end point
Visitor centre
✚ 54C2

Lunch
Take a packed lunch

Unregulated walking is not permitted in Timanfaya National Park for fear of walkers injuring themselves on the uneven terrain, or damage being caused to the fragile lichens that live on the surface of the volcanic rock. It has taken over 200 years for even this minimal flora to get established. There are two free guided walks supervised by the park authority. This, called the Tremesana Route, is the easier of the two. The Mancha Blanca Interpretation Centre itself provides a fascinating introduction to this region (➤ 58).

The walk will start or end with a short minibus ride. From Yaiza, the group starts walking near the foot of Montaña Tremesana.

In this area, figs are cultivated in stone half-circles to protect them from the wind (the trees, but not the ground they stand on, are private property).

Continue towards Caldera Rajada, ahead.

The volcano erupted from the side, splitting the mountain apart. The guide will point out amazing colours in the rocks, and explain how the eruption created hollow tubes just beneath the ground (which can be seen at close quarters at Jameos del Agua). Tell-tale signs, such as yellow sulphur stains, show the guide where these tunnels occur.

Below: *dawn over Timanfaya*
Right: *lichens eke out an existence clinging to the rocks*

The route continues between two other volcanoes, Hernández and Encantada. The guide will describe the process of plant colonisation.

The walk finally arrives at a track near the foot of a volcano called Pedro Pericó. You will be picked up by minibus and returned to the visitor centre by way of Yaiza (➤ 72).

What to See in Timanfaya National Park

✝ 54B1

✉ 3km north of Yaiza, at the foot of Timanfaya/Islote de Hilario

🕐 Daily 9–4

🍴 El Diablo restaurant (€€) at the summit

🖐 Inexpensive

↔ Islote de Hilario (➤ 20–21), Yaiza (➤ 72)

ECHADERO DE LOS CAMELLOS (CAMEL PARK) ✪

Lanzarote's camels are actually dromedaries, but nobody's quibbling over what is really just an amusement for tourists. The camel park is a corral at the foot of Timanfaya, where visitors can wait in line for a 10-minute ride up the steep, unstable slag heap of the volcano. Each animal carries two or three passengers, who are strapped into wooden seats, one perched on either side of the camel. The camel train is then led up the slope by a guide.

ISLOTE DE HILARIO (➤ 20–21, TOP TEN)

State-of-the-art displays at the Mancha Blanca visitor centre

✝ 54C2

✉ 9km from Islote de Hilario, at Mancha Blanca

☎ 928 84 08 39

🕐 Daily 9–4:45

🍴 El Diablo restaurant (€€) on the Islote de Hilario summit

🚌 None

♿ Few

🖐 Free

↔ Islote de Hilario (➤ 20–21), Ermita de los Dolores (➤ 39)

MANCHA BLANCA CENTRO DE INTERPRETACIÓN ✪✪
(INTERPRETATION CENTRE)

Located on the park boundary, near the village of Mancha Blanca, the Interpretation Centre must count as one of the park's most interesting sights – and one of the few man-made items in the landscape. The building at first appears small and low, its whiteness a sharp contrast with the dark lava. However, it turns out to be much larger, with most of the centre lying underground. Inside is a cool, calm environment of white and black surfaces and polished wood, with exhibitions about the park, a library, bookshop, and administration areas, as well as viewpoints onto the volcanic terrain. Among the most interesting exhibits is the Eruption Hall, simulating the ground movements at the time of the 1730 volcanic eruption here. Note that guides, smoking and noise are not allowed at the centre.

✝ 54B2

✉ 2km southwest of Islote de Hilario

🚌 On Ruta de los Volcanes coach tour (➤ 60)

MONTAÑA RAJADA ✪✪✪

Only to be seen on the Ruta de los Volcanes bus tour, which starts from the Islote de Hilario summit, this 350m peak gives one of the most awe-inspiring views of the park: a panoramic vista over volcanic cones and craters and the hollows caused by underground tunnels collapsing. Beyond, the blue sea makes a startling contrast.

MONTAÑA DE TIMANFAYA ✪✪✪

This, the largest of the park's volcanoes at 510m, is a vast dark cone that dominates the view throughout western Lanzarote. You can see it up close and admire the vivid red and yellow streaks (caused by mineral deposits) on the volcanoes coach tour.

✚ 54C2
✉ 1km southwest of Islote de Hilario
🚌 On Ruta de los Volcanes coach tour (➤ 60)

PLAYA DE LA MADERA ✪

Where the park meets the sea there are many inaccessible coves and black sand beaches. One, however can be reached by car on a track that is marked – very truthfully – Camino en Mal Estado (track in poor condition). The track can be reached from Tinajo, Mancha Blanca or a turn close to the Islote de Hilario entrance.

✚ 28A3
✉ 10km northwest of Mancha Blanca
🚌 None

The malpaís meets the sea: the Timanfaya coast

TIMANFAYA PLAIN ✪✪✪

The flat lowland that lies at the foot of the volcanoes is a sea of dark jagged rock, resembling coal cinders. The terrain is so unusual that it deserves a good look.

✚ 28B2
✉ Between Yaiza and park entrance

VALLE DE LA TRANQUILIDAD (VALLEY OF TRANQUILLITY) ✪✪✪

In this part of the park some tiny bushes are trying to grow and a few tufts of grey-looking grasses manage to cling to the slopes, a hint of the future greenery that may one day take hold here.

✚ 54C2
✉ 1km south of Islote de Hilario
🚌 On Ruta de los Volcanes coach tour

Timanfaya Drive

Distance
30km, including 14km coach trip

Time
About 2 hours
Last coach trip at 5PM

Start point
Yaiza
 28B2

End point
Mancha Blanca
28B3

Lunch
Restaurante El Diablo (€€)
Islote de Hilario
928 84 00 57

This drive crosses the *malpaís*, or badlands, and includes the official coach tour, which offers the only way to see the most awesome region at the heart of the park. The *Ruta de los Volcanes* coach tour departs at roughly hourly intervals throughout the day from outside the El Diablo restaurant on the summit of Islote de Hilario. The trip is included in the Islote entrance ticket.

From Yaiza drive due north on the Tinajo road. The dark, awesome malpaís *of Timanfaya Plain (➤ 59) starts almost at once. After 3km, the Camel Park (➤ 58) appears beside the road on the left. A further 4km brings you to the ticket booth for Islote de Hilario (➤ 20–21). There can be long queues here. Park at the summit of Islote de Hilario. Having watched the wardens demonstrate the intense heat of the earth just below the surface, take the coach trip*

around the centre of the 18th-century volcanic eruptions.

Although geared to tourists, and with certain special effects on board – designed to conjure up the atmosphere and power of the volcanic activity – you're unlikely to be disappointed by this extraordinary and memorable drive.

The coach takes a winding narrow road to Montaña Rajada (➤ 58), one of the most impressive viewpoints, looking out across volcanic cones, collapsed underground tunnels and utter devastation reaching to the sea.

Manrique's volcano-top restaurant blends into the dramatic scenery

The landscape is not all dark – there are vivid colours in and around the volcanic cones. Below is the Valley of Tranquillity (➤ 59), which was buried in a downpour of volcanic particles.

Left: *some vegetation manages to survive in Valle de la Tranquilidad*

The bus skirts Timanfaya itself, and several smaller volcanoes, before returning to Islote de Hilario. After walking and exploring in the small area permitted around the Islote, continue to Mancha Blanca on the main road.

At Mancha Blanca visit the Interpretation Centre (➤ 58) and the Hermitage of Our Lady of Sorrows (➤ 39), a contrast between the scientific and spiritual aspects of the volcanoes' power.

➕ 29D4
✉ Guinate (4km from Haría)
☎ 928 83 55 00
🕐 Daily 10–5
🚍 Join an excursion organised from your resort, or go by car
♿ None
💷 Expensive
↔ Haría (➤ 42), Mirador del Río (➤ 24)

➕ 28A1
✉ 35km from Arrecife
🍴 Bars and snack bars (€) and restaurants (€–€€) on the promenade
🚍 No 6 from Arrecife or Puerto del Carmen to Playa Blanca. There are frequent departures daily, and the journey takes either 35 minutes or an hour. depending on the route
⛴ To Corralejo, on Fuerteventura, several times daily. There are also ferries to Lobos Island, in between the two larger islands.
ℹ Calle Varadero ☎ 928 51 90 18
♿ Few
↔ Timanfaya National Park (➤ 55–61), Los Hervideros (➤ 43), El Golfo (➤ 41), Águila (➤ 36)
❓ A new coastal walkway from town goes east to Playa de las Coloradas (2km) and west to the lighthouse at Punta de Pechiguera (2km).

PARQUE TROPICAL (TROPICAL PARK) ✪

The Tropical Park on the steep hillside behind the peaceful village of Guinate in the north of the island is an enjoyable and entertaining birdlife centre with over 300 species to see. The parrot shows are a particular treat.

PLAYA BLANCA ✪✪✪

This purpose-built – and fast-growing – resort on the island's southern shore basks in a sheltered position where both the wind and the waves are subdued.

The town's golden, sandy main beach catches the sun, is perfectly protected from the breeze, and is backed (in town) by an attractive promenade with plenty of greenery and café tables. There are two smaller beaches east of the centre, and another attractive beach area west of the port.

For the moment, Playa Blanca remains a quiet little place, with an away-from-it-all feeling that belies the fact that it is only 15km on a fast road across the Rubicón plain to Yaiza, and is therefore very conveniently placed for visiting Timanfaya National Park and all the sights of the southern half of the island. It's also handy for the west coast, where the volcanic *malpaís* reaches down to the Atlantic breakers.

From Playa Blanca's seashore you can look across the 11km channel between Lanzarote and Fuerteventura for a clear view of Fuerteventura and, in front of it, the small dark volcanic shape of Isla de Lobos. Ferries cross to Fuerteventura several times a day from Playa Blanca's main harbour for an easy and enjoyable day excursion. Fishing boats use the harbour too, and restaurants along the promenade feature plenty of freshly caught fish. There's also the popular Marina Rubicón, which has some shops and great waterside bars and restaurants.

The harbour area and the few streets to the east were the only part of Playa Blanca that existed before tourism

took off here recently. West of the harbour, linked to it by another promenade, there is another development of shops, restaurants and accommodation, round a sheltered little bay of fine sand and gentle waters.

Playa Blanca is the furthest south of Lanzarote's resorts, a relatively long way from the sights in the north, but it has some clear advantages for those who want sun, sea and sand, good food and a peaceful atmosphere. With almost nothing here before the resort was built, it is dedicated to holiday enjoyment. Most entertainment is provided by the hotels, which in Playa Blanca are of a high standard. Set back from the promenade, attractive holiday apartment complexes and imaginatively designed, good-quality modern hotels are just a few paces from the sea.

Many visitors search out the secluded sandy beaches to the east and west, including impressive Playa Papagayo (► 50). To get your bearings, follow the coast round to the lonely clifftop Castillo de las Coloradas, which can be seen from anywhere in Playa Blanca. From here, in a sweep of coast, the great sandy bays of Papagayo can be glimpsed between the headlands that stretch to Punta de Papagayo. The easiest way to visit the more remote beaches is to hire a small boat from the harbour at Maga Blanca.

The central beach in Playa Blanca is backed by an attractive modern promenade

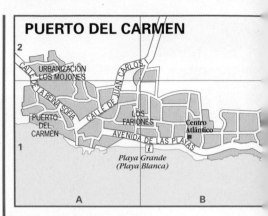

PUERTO DEL CARMEN

Tuck into freshly caught fish at one of the local restaurants round the harbour

Puerto del Carmen

Lanzarote's main resort is surprisingly small and low-key. Yet it offers everything for a satisfying holiday: 5km of broad pale sand beaches, a wide choice of places to eat and stay, and an excellent base for reaching all the other sights of the island.

Puerto del Carmen is almost entirely a new town, a narrow strip clinging to the beach and dedicated to tourism. To the north it spreads out towards the airport and Arrecife, while at the other end of town the original fishing harbour lies south of the main beach. César Manrique's preoccupation with traditional, white, single-storey dwellings is less evident in tourist resorts, yet Puerto del Carmen has tried in its way to remain faithful to him. There are no high-rise structures, and almost all buildings, new or old, are white and unpretentious, even if they are not especially pretty or traditional in the way that Manrique might have preferred.

What to see in Puerto del Carmen

OLD HARBOUR ✪✪✪

The small fishing harbour just south of Playa Grande was the heart of the original Puerto del Carmen village. It's still very much in use today, and gives character to this part of town; in the square next to the port, you can watch the locals playing *boules*. The local restaurants serve excellent fresh fish.

64A1
Western edge of town
Seafood restaurants (€–€€) around the harbour
No 2 from Arrecife stops on Avenida de las Playas
Few

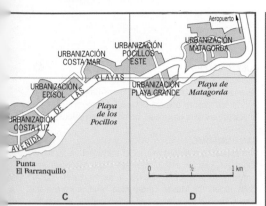

Below: *relaxing on Playa Grande*

PLAYA GRANDE (PLAYA BLANCA) ✪✪✪

The town's main beach of yellow sand runs alongside busy Avenida de las Playas, the main artery of the town. Confusingly, it is often referred to as Playa Blanca, the same name as a separate resort at the southern tip of the island. On the beach side of the Avenida there's an attractive paved walkway with palm trees; across the street is a long strip of bars and restaurants, tourist shops and places of entertainment. After dark, the Centro Atlántico along here is *the* place for clubbing and nightlife. The tourist office is by the beach. The promenade leads to Pocillos and Matagorda beaches, and continues as a coastal walkway to Arrecife.

🖪 64A1
🛈 Avenida de las Playas
☎ 928 51 33 51
🍴 Restaurants (€€) on Avenida de las Playas
🚍 No 2 from Arrecife every 20 minutes (30 minutes Sat–Sun)

PLAYA DE LOS POCILLOS ✪

With a vast, sandy beach 2km from the centre of town, Pocillos is much quieter and less crowded, with some above-average accommodation. The northern end of Pocillos beach is an appealing stretch with good restaurants and shops, called Los Jameos Playa – also the name of an excellent hotel here.

🖪 65C1
🍴 Restaurants (€) at CC Jameos Playa
🚍 Buses from Arrecife approx every half hour

PLAYA DE MATAGORDA ✪

About 4km from town along the promenade, Matagorda has few attractions and feels remote. However (apart from daytime aircraft noise) it is tranquil and traffic-free, with a section of sandy beach and a shopping centre.

🖪 65D1
🍴 CC Matagorda (€)
🚍 Buses to Puerto del Carmen and Arrecife

PUERTO CALERO

The island's best marina and the starting point for many catamaran and submarine trips, Puerto Calero is worth a visit for its recently opened Cetacean Museum. There are Interactive exhibits on whales, porpoises and dolphins.

SAN BARTLOMÉ

This appealing country town, all in traditional black, white and green, has the simple style that César Manrique was fighting to preserve. Down a side street, Calle Constitución, the **Museo Etnográfico Tanit**, in a grand old house, displays the island's unique folk culture. Its eclectic assortment of photos, paintings, furniture, winemaking paraphenalia, clothing, tools, kitchenware, religious artefacts and more inspire admiration for the history and heritage of the local people. Behind the courtyard stands a tiny, richly decorated private chapel, and a garden.

SALINAS DE JANUBIO

At several places around the island shallow seawater lagoons have been transformed into salt pans. The most productive of these is at Janubio, on the southern edge of Timanfaya National Park. The large salty lagoon, enclosed by hills, has been divided into neat rectangles subdivided into hundreds of smaller squares. As the water evaporates it leaves behind large quantities of salt used in the island's traditional fish processing and preserving industries.

Did you know ?

Lanzarote's salt pans traditionally played a surprising role in the islanders' health. Because farming was so difficult, fish became essential in the diet. But because fish were impossible to keep in the hot climate, dried and salted fish became important. Hence the salt pans – and the local speciality sancocho, *a stew of salt fish.*

LA SANTA ⭐

La Santa is a popular little village in the middle of the wilder, less populous north coast, and is well placed for a lunch stop. It overlooks the curious low-lying peninsula known as La Isleta, which lies about 2km east of the village, cut off from the mainland only at very high tides. To reach the island, simply continue on the road past the entrance to Club La Santa.

La Isleta is home to one of the world's top private residential sports resorts, called Club La Santa: the facilities are available only as part of a full package holiday.

TEGUISE (▶ 25, TOP TEN)

✚ 28B3
🍴 Fresh-fish restaurants (€) in village
🚌 No 16 runs between Arrecife and La Santa eight times a day Mon–Fri, three to five times Sat–Sun. It takes about an hour each way
♿ None
↔ Famara (▶ 40), Ermita de los Dolores (▶ 39)

The geometric Janubio salt pans produce salt for dried fish

In the Know

To get a real flavour of the islands, here are some ideas:

(**L** = on Lanzarote; **F** = on Fuerteventura)

Ways to Be a Local

Eat *tapas*, which should be nibbled with an aperitif as a starter, or during the long hours between lunch and dinner. Eat lunch at 2 and dinner at 9 or 10.

Take a siesta. Life starts early and continues till late. Locals don't doze on a sun lounger all afternoon but they do take a few quiet hours after lunch.

Dress with respect. Older islanders do not strip off in the sun. Most won't even wear shorts, but prefer neat dresses or trousers, and short sleeves. Many men wear a jacket even on hot days..

Drink espresso. Locals almost never drink milky coffee. At most, they have just a dash of milk – that's a *café cortado*. It's OK, though, to have a *café con leche* (coffee with milk) for breakfast.

Enjoy tasty snacks or a drink in a friendly local tapas bar

Spice things up with a touch of *mojo*. A flavoursome sauce served with a number of dishes. It's a Canarian speciality so choose *mojo rojo* if you like it hot or *mojo verde* if have cooler tastes.

Shout every word in a bar, bang the counter with coins and loudly call an already harrassed barman – in Spanish, of course. If you aren't a native, and don't have fluent Spanish, however, it might be better to be quiet and polite.

Knock the other islands. On Lanzarote, say that Fuerteventura is barren and windy. On Fuerteventura, sneer about Lanzarote's manicured beaches and elaborate attractions. On either island, tell everyone how overdeveloped and rainy most of the other Canaries are.

Forget about flamenco. Although tourist venues put on shows for guests, clichéd Spanish traditions like flamenco and bullfighting are not part of Canary Islands culture.

Buy a lottery ticket. These are sold by locals with disabilities, and buying is almost compulsory.

Never sunbathe. Locals stay out of the sun. On an especially fine spring day, a man might remove his jacket and sit outdoors – in the shade.

Good Places to Have Lunch

L Bodega El Chupadero (€€)
 Signposted off the LZ30, opposite the Ermita La Geria, La Asomada ☎ 928 17 31 15 . In the heart of the vineyards of La Geria, but worth the effort to find it. It's a comfy tapas bar with friendly staff and delicious food.

L Casal Cura (€€)
✉ Encamación Rodríguez 1, Haria ☎ 928 83 55 56. In the north of the island is one of Lanzarote's best restaurants, offering several local stews like *sancocho*, *puchero* and *potaje*.

L Castillo de San José (€€)
✉ Castillo de San José, Arrecife ☎ 928 81 23 21. The restaurant of Lanzarote's modern art gallery, inside an oceanside 15th-century fortress, is a typical example of César Manrique's imaginative style. Black tables, white walls and good local dishes.

L El Diablo (€€)
✉ Islote de Hilario, Parque Nacional de Timanfaya

☎ 928 84 00 57. At the summit of the Islote de Hilario with wonderful panoramic views, and traditional Canarian cuisine cooked over heat rising directly from the earth.

L La Longa (€–€€)
✉ Calle Varadero.
☎ 928 51 13 77. In the midst of Puerto del Carmen's Old Port, this unpretentious restaurant is a big busy quayside fried fish bar packed with locals.

L Los Helechos (€–€€)
✉ At the viewpoint 5km south of Haría ☎ 928 83 58 17. Here you can feast on the superb view as much as the fresh fish and popular Canarian dishes.

F La Marquesina (€€)
✉ Muelle Chico, Corralejo, Fuerteventura ☎ 928 53 54 35. At the harbour. Relaxed and unpretentious place popular with locals. Fresh fish a speciality.

L Mesón La Jordana (€€€)
✉ Calle Los Geranios, Costa Teguise ☎ 928 59 03 28. La Jordana gives a local flavour to some international cooking.

F Casa Santa María (€€–€€€)
✉ Plaza Santa María de Betancuría 1, Betancuría ☎ 928 87 80 36. This bar-restaurant, in a rustic 16th-century house with local character, offers excellent Canarian cooking.

Fariones (€)
✉ Calle La Quemadita
☎ 928 84 25 31. Sample some good-value seafood at this simple restaurant by Orzola's little harbour.

5

Top Activities

Tan: even in January there's an average of 8 hours sunshine per day. It's more in every other month. There's no better place to enjoy it than the islands' huge sandy beaches.

Windsurf: great beaches and stiff breezes create ideal conditions, especially on the coasts of Fuerteventura's Corralejo (➤ 80) and Jandía peninsula (➤ 84).

Dunewalk: walking on Fuerteventura's vast dunes is more like an expedition in a desert than a stroll on the beach (➤ 18).

Discover Manrique: his influence is all over Lanzarote, but the best place to experience his work is at his former home, the Fundacíon César Manrique (➤ 19).

Get into volcanoes: learn all about them at the Mancha Blanca Visitor Centre (➤ 58)

Stylish menu card from La Era restaurant

Corralejo Beach, Fuerteventura

and see them in the Timanfaya National Park (➤ 55–61).

10

Top Beaches

F Playa Barlovento (➤ 85), western Jandía, Fuerteventura – vast empty sands, not for swimming

L Playa Dorada, at Playa Blanca – delightful sandy beach shelving into sheltered bay, perfect for swimming and sunbathing.

L Playa de las Conchas, Isla Graciosa (➤ 44), off Lanzarote

F Playas de Corralejo (➤ 80), Corralejo, Fuerteventura – 10km long, backed by huge dunes

L Playa Famara (➤ 40), northwest Lanzarote, backed by high cliffs

L Playa Mujeres, nr Playa Blanca (➤ 62), Lanzarote

L Playa Papagayo (➤ 50–51), near Playa Blanca, Lanzarote

L Playa de los Pocillos (➤ 65), an immense sweep of sand, popular for sunbathing and swimming.

F Playa de Sotavento (➤ 84), Jandía Peninsula, Fuerteventura – gorgeous, 30km-long sweep of sand.

L Puerto del Carmen (➤ 64–66), Lanzarote – the island's main resort with a great beach, Playa Grande.

Southern Lanzarote

Distance
70km

Time
5 hours

Start/end point
Arrecife
➕ 29C2

Lunch
Take a picnic or, on Sundays, enjoy a meal at Casona de Yaiza (€€€),
✉ Calle El Rincón 11, Yaiza
☎ 928 83 62 62

This is a fascinating and enjoyable day out, taking in the island's extraordinary variety and some of its most exceptional sights.

From the Arrecife city ring road (Circunvalación) take the turn to San Bartolomé (➤ 66). Stay on this rural road until you reach the junction with the road to Uga and Yaiza, on the left.

At this junction, close to the very centre of Lanzarote, is Manriqué's strange cubist monument to the *campesino*, or peasant (➤ 45). Beside it is a small rural museum. Mozaga, straight ahead, has a good *bodega* (wine cellar), where you can buy local wines.

Take the Uga and Yaiza road. Beware – it becomes narrow, with deep ditches on each side. Passing is difficult in places.

This road enters La Geria, where vines grow in hollows dug into bleak grey volcanic desert. After 13km it reaches the attractive village of Uga (➤ 72).

At a junction, turn right for Yaiza, just 3km away.

Pretty white Yaiza (➤ 72–73) lies on the edge of the dark *malpaís*. Stop in the village for a walk and perhaps lunch.

Continue through Yaiza on the main Playa Blanca road.

After some 3km, on the right beside a junction, are the strange geometric salt pans of Janubio (➤ 66).

The road soon begins to cross the flat, rather bleak Rubicón plain. Follow it right into the resort of Playa Blanca (➤ 62–63).

Spend an agreeable half-hour on the promenade of this small, modern beach resort. For a bigger beach, and fewer people, explore Papagayo, down a coastal track east of town (➤ 50–51).

Take the less-frequented, minor road 6km

northeast towards Femés (➤ 40). Continue another 6km to the main road and turn right for Puerto del Carmen.

The road winds steeply down into Puerto del Carmen (➤ 64–65), a lively, pleasant family resort, with a big beach backed by restaurants.

Take the main road past the airport and back into Arrecife.

César Manrique loved the traditional, low, white-painted houses of Yaiza

★ 28B2
✉ 17km west of Arrecife
🚌 No 6 (Arrecife–Playa
   Blanca)
♿ Few
↔ Yaiza (➤ 72–73), La
   Geria (➤ 26), Timanfaya
   National Park (➤ 55–61)

Above: *a camel train
returns to Uga from
Timanfaya*

★ 28B2
✉ 15km from Playa Blanca,
   around 20km from
   Arrecife
🚌 No 6 runs frequently
   between Arrecife and
   Playa Blanca
♿ Few
↔ Timanfaya National Park
   (➤ 55–61), Islote de
   Hilario (➤ 20–21), Salinas
   de Janubio (➤ 66), Uga
   (➤ 72), La Geria (➤ 26)
❓ Horse riding tours begin
   here

UGA ✪

An incongruously green and fertile wine village on the fringes of the desolate volcanic terrain of the Timanfaya National Park, Uga stands at the western end of the bizarre La Geria vineyard area, where the vines grow in volcanic rubble.

Despite the awesome location, Uga's simple single-storey white dwellings give it a neat, rather African charm. One of its main activities is breeding camels: not only do the animals that carry tourists up Islote de Hilario come from here, but also those that are used for safaris on the island.

If you want to see La Geria, drive out of Uga on the road to San Bartolomé via Mozaga, La Geria's main town and principal outlet for the region's wines. Be warned that in places the road becomes rough and very narrow.

VALLE DE LA GERIA (➤ 26, TOP TEN)

YAIZA ✪✪

This arty, yet unpretentious, picturesque old village of palm trees and dazzling whiteness has often been described as one of the prettiest villages in the Canary Islands. It is dramatically located, facing golden hills one way, barren blackness the other. Standing on the very edge of the malpaís, it was all but destroyed in the Timanfaya volcanic eruptions of 1730–36. Just a handful of houses survived, but, as many surrounding fields and gardens were left intact, villagers gradually returned and rebuilt their homes.

The sunshine reflects brilliantly off their simple white-washed walls and houses. Some of the buildings look prosperous and dignified, with little balconies and pleasing, flower-filled gardens. These were once the homes of wealthy 19th-century merchants who settled in the village. Combining charm and elegance it's no real surprise that César Marique wanted the whole island to look like this.

Did you know ?

Yaiza, standing on the edge of the malpaís, was almost entirely destroyed by Timanfaya's eruptions of 1730–36, and 11 smaller villages were wiped off the map. Yet despite the utter devastation wreaked by Lanzarote's volcanoes, it is thought that no one on the island has ever been injured during a volcanic eruption.

Below: *an elegant rural hotel at Yaiza*

While in the village, pop into the 18th-century church whose tower rises over the main square, Plaza de los Remedios, and visit the municipal art gallery at the Casa de Cultura or the Galería Yaiza art gallery. The latter exhibits local paintings and ceramics. Most of the work on show is for sale so this is a great opportunity to pick up a unique and stylish souvenir.

Fuerteventura

A wild, unkempt golden desert island of
sunshine and sand, Fuerteventura looks like a
fragment of the Sahara. Visitors exploring it find
only light, peace, rocks of red and yellow and black, and wide
open spaces. The sands have indeed blown here from the
Sahara, on the strong winds that give the island its name.
Even so, eastern Fuerteventura is sheltered, though these
coasts are famous for their windsurfing. In the interior and
west, higher cones and ridges of darker rocks and vivid
colours show the island's volcanic origin, though there hasn't
been a murmur from these eroded volcanoes for thousands of
years. Overall there's a sense that nothing at all has changed
here in a long time.

> '... *an oasis in the desert*
> *that is civilisation.* '

DON MIGUEL UNAMUNO
(banished to Fuerteventura in 1924)

———————•———————

Vast tracks of rippled dunes stretch down the coast from Corralejo

LANZAROTE & FUERTEVENTURA

0   20   40   60   80 km

LANZAROTE

Isla de Alegranza

Isla Graciosa

Arrecife

Playa Blanca

Corralejo

Puerto del Rosario

FUERTEVENTURA

Las Palmas de Gran Canaria

GRAN CANARIA

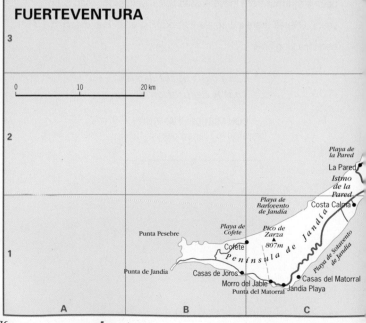

FUERTEVENTURA

3

0   10   20 km

2

Playa de la Pared

La Pared

Istmo de la Pared

Playa de Barlovento de Jandía

Costa Calma

Playa de Cofete

Pico de Zarza
807m

Peninsula de Jandía

Playa de Sotavento de Jandía

Punta Pesebre

Cofete

Punta de Jandía

Casas de Joros

Morro del Jable

Punta del Matorral

Jandía Playa

Casas del Matorral

1

A   B   C

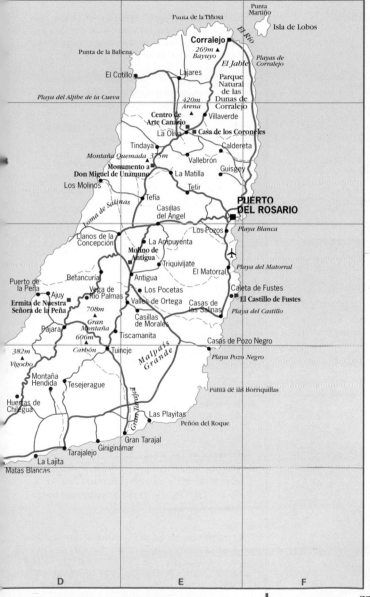

Punta
Martiño
Isla de Lobos

Punta de la Tiñosa

El Río

Corralejo
269m ▲
Bayuyo

Playas de
Corralejo

Punta de la Ballena

El Jable

El Cotillo

Lajares

Parque
Natural
de las
Dunas de
Corralejo

Playa del Aljibe de la Cueva

420m
Arena ▲

Centro de
Arte Canario

● Villaverde

La Oliva ● ■ **Casa de los Coroneles**

Tindaya ●

Caldereta ●

Montaña Quemada 375m

Vallebrón ●

Monumento a
Don Miguel de Unamuno

La Matilla ●

Guisguey ●

Los Molinos ●

Tefía ●

Tetir ●

Loma de Salinas

Casillas
del Ángel ●

PUERTO
DEL ROSARIO ■

Llanos de la
Concepción ●

La Ampuyenta ●

Los Pozos ●

Playa Blanca

Molino de
Antigua ●

Triquivijate ●

✈

Betancuria ●

Antigua ●

El Matorral ●

Playa del Matorral

Puerto de
la Peña ●

Vega de
Río Palmas ●

Ajuy ●

● Los Pocetas

Caleta de Fustes ●

Ermita de Nuestra
Señora de la Peña ■

Valles de Ortega ●

Casas de
las Salinas ●

■ **El Castillo de Fustes**

Playa del Castillo

708m
▲
Gran
Montaña

Casillas
de Morales ●

Pájara ●

606m

Tiscamanita ●

Casas de Pozo Negro

382m
▲
Vigocho

Carbón

Tuineje ●

Malpaís
Grande

Playa Pozo Negro

Montaña
Hendida ●

Tesejerague ●

Punta de las Borriquillas

Huertas de
Chilegua ●

Gran Tarajal

Las Playitas ●

Peñón del Roque

Tarajalejo ●

Giniginámar ●

Gran Tarajal ●

La Lajita ●

Matas Blancas

D   E   F

Northern Fuerteventura

Distance
115km

Time
3–4hrs

Start/end point
Corralejo
🕂 77E5

Lunch
La Flor de Antigua (€€)
✉ Carretera General de
Betancuria 43, Antigua
☎ 928 87 81 68
🕐 Lunch, dinner. Closed
Sun

*Carving around the
doorway of Betancuría's
interesting church*

This drive passes through uninhabited areas of awesome space and emptiness, yet also fertile corners and picturesque villages. The main roads are good, but there's nowhere to buy petrol, so start out with a full tank.

From Corralejo take Route 600 due south into the interior, turning right after 7km at the first turning, which goes to Lajares.

Lajares, a pretty village of white cottages, is noted for its embroidery and other traditional handicrafts.

Take the road to La Oliva, to a landscape of volcanic malpaís. On the left rises the soaring sandy mountain of Montaña Arena. The road reaches Route 600 again at La Oliva.

The agreeable village of La Oliva (▶ 87) brings together the island's history and its variety of imposing terrain.

Follow the road south, passing Montaña Tindaya on the right. Carry on to the junction at the foot of the dark volcano Montaña Quemada, 'Burnt Mountain'. The Unamuno memorial (▶ 87) can be seen from the road. Turn right towards Betancuria. At a T-junction, keep right across a plain, passing several windmills. Continue into hills, climbing up before winding sharply down into Betancuria.

Betancuria (▶ 79) has several interesting old buildings and deserves a leisurely stroll.

Return up the steep hill road to take the turn for Antigua (▶ 79), on the right. After exploring Antigua, visit the restored windmills on the main road on the way north to Puerto del Rosario (▶ 89). Turn onto the coast road north towards Corralejo.

The road crosses stony terrain for some 10km before reaching El Jable, a thrilling landscape of pale dunes designated as a Natural Park (▶ 18). Out to sea is the little island of Lobos (▶ 86). The road continues into Corralejo.

ANTIGUA ⊙⊙

Antigua dates back to 1485 and the early colonial period. Around the village much of Fuerteventura's historic character has been preserved. In the surrounding countryside windmills (*molinos*) still make use of the continual breezes to grind corn for *gofio*, the roasted, milled cereal that is a staple Canarian food. The 200-year-old El Molino, on the main road heading north from the village, has been restored and converted into a delightful cultural and crafts centre, the **Centro de Artesanía Molino de Antigua**, with a craft shop, garden with palm and cactus, and galleries housing temporary exhibitions.

🚩 77E3
✉ 21km southwest of Puerto del Rosario
🍴 La Flor de Antigua (€€)
☎ 928 87 81 68
🚌 No 1 from Puerto del Rosario to Morro Jable six times daily
♿ None
↔ Betancuria (➤ 79)
❓ 8 September is the Fiesta of Our Lady of Antigua

Centro de Artesanía Molino de Antigua
☎ 928 87 80 41
🕐 Tue–Sat 10–6
💰 Inexpensive

Antigua's handsome 18th-century church also boasts a pretty garden

BETANCURIA ⊙⊙⊙

Named after the 15th-century Norman conqueror of this island, Jean de Béthencourt – Juan de Betancuria in Spanish – this bright white village in the very centre of Fuerteventura remained its capital until 1834. Betancuría still keeps something of its historic, aristocratic character. De Béthencourt built his capital here in the belief that being so far from the sea, it would be safe from the Moorish pirates who terrorised the coasts. He was proved wrong; pirates repeatedly sacked the town, in 1593 destroying the original Norman-style cathedral and taking away 600 captives as slaves.

The church was rebuilt in 1620, in an interesting hybrid style, with a painted ceiling, a fine baroque altarpiece and ancient gravestones forming part of the floor. It became a cathedral again in 1924. Many village houses still have façades and doorways dating from the 1500s and 1600s. Across the church square, a museum devoted to religious art displays de Béthencourt's original standard, the Pendón de la Conquista. A **museum of archaeology**, across the (usually dry) river, houses Guanche relics, which are exceptionally plentiful here.

🚩 77D3
✉ 28km southwest of Puerto del Rosario
🍴 Simple bar-restaurant (€) beside Casa Museo; Restaurant Casa de Santa Maria (€€€), by church
🚌 No 2 from Puerto del Rosario to Vega de Río Palma, twice a day Mon–Sat
↔ Ermita de Nuestra Señora de la Peña (➤ 81), Antigua (➤ 79)
❓ The major local saint's day is San Buenaventura, 14 July

Museo Arqueológico
✉ Calle Roberto Roldán 12–14
☎ 928 87 82 41
🕐 Tue–Sat 10–6
💰 Inexpensive

🞤 77E3
✉ 12km south of Puerto del Rosario

🍴 Restaurants (€–€€)

🚌 No 3 from Puerto del Rosario to Caleta de Fustes, via airport every 30 mins Mon–Sat, every hour on Sun

↔ Puerto del Rosario (➤ 89)

Above: *fishing in Corralejo Harbour*

🞤 77E5
✉ 30km north of Puerto del Rosario

🍴 Wide choice of restaurants (€–€€)

🚌 No 6 via Puerto del Rosario, every 30 mins Mon–Fri, hourly Sat–Sun

⛴ To Isla de Lobos (10 minutes, ☎ 928 86 62 38); to Playa Blanca on Lanzarote (20 minutes one way, Fred Olsen Line ☎ 928 53 50 90).

ℹ Plaza Pública ☎ 928 86 62 35

↔ Isla de Lobos (➤ 86), La Oliva (➤ 87)

CALETA DE FUSTES ★

This popular, fast-growing resort area receives large numbers of package tourists in mainly budget accommodation, having the advantage (or disadvantage) of being close to the airport. Several mid-quality small hotels and low-rise budget apartments have been built here recently and more are going up. There's a very good golden beach, a few lively bars and several inexpensive eating places. An 18th-century fortified round tower of dark stone, called simply El Castillo – the castle – stands next to a small marina and has become part of a beach complex with restaurant, bars, watersports hire facilities, and a supermarket.

CORRALEJO ★★★

Though still a working fishing harbour and a pleasant small town, this is Fuerteventura's biggest and most accessible beach resort. Lying on the breezy northern tip of the island, just across the narrow strait from tourist developments on the southern tip of Lanzarote, Corralejo has woken up to the fact that it too has that magic formula 'sun, sea and sand'. As a consequence, several hotels and apartment complexes have opened. For sun, its record can hardly be matched anywhere else in the Canaries. When it comes to sand, although the white beach in town is not very large, immense golden beaches and mountainous dunes stretch out just behind the town and go on for miles (➤ 18). The heart of the town centres on a bustling square with shops, bars and budget restaurants, and there is a more lively nightlife than in other resorts on Fuerteventura.

EL COTILLO ✪

This small holiday development around a fishing harbour on the windy west coast near La Oliva has black cliffs, sandy beaches, watersports and an 18th-century fortification called the Torre del Tostón or Castillo de Rico Roque. The air's fresh and clean and, though it's a popular excursion destination, there's an away-from-it-all feeling. Windsurfers like the wild waves at the southern beach; families and sunbathers prefer the gentler northern beach.

🚩	77E5
✉	20km south of Corralejo
🍴	Simple restaurants (€) near the harbour
🚌	No 8 to Corralejo every two hours Mon–Sat; No 7 three times a day Mon–Sat to Puerto del Rosario

ERMITA DE NUESTRA SEÑORA DE LA PEÑA ✪✪

Tucked away in the hills outside Vega de Río Palma, just south of Betancuria is this remote, whitewashed hermitage. It's hard to reach, and getting there involves some stiff walking. The tiny building houses an alabaster statue of the revered patron saint of Fuerteventura. The third Saturday in September is her feast day, which brings crowds of islanders here for the all-important *romería*, afascinating annual pilgrimage and procession.

🚩	77D3
✉	5km south of Betancuría on the Pájara road
🕐	Tue–Sun 11–1 and 5–7, closed Mon
🚌	No 2 from Puerto del Rosario to Vega de Río Palma twice daily

GRAN TARAJAL ✪

Tarajal is the Canary tamarisk, numbers of which give a green aspect to this area and the valley of Gran Tarajal behind. Here on a south-facing shore, dark hills reach the sea at this small, charmless harbour village, which claims to be Fuerteventura's second-largest town. Unusually for the island, the beaches have black sand. As well as tamarisk, the valley is noted for its date palms, which produce not only fruit, but also the raw materials for the island's ubiquitous straw hats and basketwork. Las Playas (or Las Playitas), a short drive up the coast, is another growing new development.

🚩	77E2
✉	45km south of Puerto del Rosario
🍴	Cafés and restaurants (€–€€) on the beachfront
🚌	No 1 from Puerto del Rosario to Morro Jable stops here, about six times daily
⇄	Tuineje (► 89)
❓	Candlemas, on 2 Feb, is a big fiesta here, celebrated as the Fiesta Nuestra Señora de la Candelaria

---

Did you know ?

Now least inhabited of the Canaries (in terms of population per square metre), in Guanche times Fuerteventura was one of the most populous. It has more Guanche relics and sites than any of the other Canary islands. Though not always easily accessible, sites are scattered over a wide area, generally unmonitored, with free access. Tourist maps usually show them.

Food & Drink

Contrary to popular belief, food in the Canaries does not consist mainly of pizza, pasta and paella. For visitors who want to experience the real character and gastronomy of Lanzarote and Fuerteventura, there's plenty of indigenous food to be enjoyed. While the informal eateries in beach resorts do unsurprisingly tend to focus on international favourites, most inland restaurants offer traditional local cuisine. Look out for the word *tipíco*, which roughly means 'traditional' or 'local'.

Malvasia
While other Canary Islands may produce wine, few can compete with Lanzarote's fine malvasia. Made of the grape that normally produces malmsey, Lanzarote's version – from the volcanic vineyards of La Geria – doesn't taste of fire and brimstone, as you might suspect, but has a delicious crisp fruity dryness, full of light and flavour.

Mojo

One of the most genuinely Canarian words on the menu is *mojo*. Meat, fish and vegetables may all be served *con mojo* – with *mojo* – the piquant sauce that comes in different versions, more or less spicy according to what it accompanies. The two main types are *mojo verde*, green *mojo*, made with parsley and coriander giving a cool, sharp flavour, and *mojo rojo*, the spicier, red sauce made with chillis and peppers.

Gofio

The other most distinctively Canarian food is *gofio*. This staple of the Guanche diet is still very much in use. A rough roasted wholemeal flour (usually of maize, but possibly also of barley, wheat, or even chickpeas), it appears in soups, as a sort of polenta, as a paste mixed with vegetables, or as breads, cakes and puddings. *Flan gofio*, which resembles semolina pudding, has interesting African undertones. The people of Lanzarote and Fuerteventura are fond of hearty meat stews – sometimes with misleading names like Lanzarote's *potaje de berros* (watercress soup), in which the greenery may be barely discernible! Such rich, savoury soup-stews, usually combining several meats, including pork and rabbit, with chickpeas and vegetables and often thickened with *gofio*, are the main speciality; *rancho canario* and *puchero* (similar to French cassoulet) are typical, and especially popular for Sunday lunch. *El cocido* is Fuerteventura's version of these traditional Canarian *garbanzos*

Freshly caught fish on the Corralejo quayside

Dried fish, prepared in the Canary Islands for as long as they've been inhabited, is still popular today

Cheese
Cheesemaking may be considered as not just production of a staple food, but as a local craft. Especially on Fuerteventura, the islanders are proud of their traditional Majorero cheese.

compuestos (chickpea stew). Rabbit, *conejo*, is an especially popular and inexpensive ingredient on Lanzarote.

Vegetables & Fish

Vegetarians beware – *potaje*, vegetable stew, usually contains some meat. Fish soups include the well-known Canarian *sancocho*, a thick stew of salted fish and vegetables. Start your meal with *gambas al ajillo*, shrimps in garlic-rich olive oil, or *pulpo*, octopus. Main dishes tend to be plain and simple, such as grilled or fried fresh fish.

Thanks in part to the obvious difficulties of cultivation in this volcanic landscape, vegetables don't feature strongly in local specialities. But there are notable exceptions, in particular *cebollas* (onions); *batatas* (sweet potatoes) and tasty small *papas* (the local name for potatoes), which usually appear as *papas arrugadas con mojo*. Literally 'wrinkly potatoes', these are delectable new potatoes cooked in their skins with plenty of salt until the water has completely boiled away, sometimes served with a heavy sprinkling of crunchy rock salt – and *mojo*. Eat them by hand. *Batatas con mojo*, sweet potatoes in hot sauce, are an interesting alternative.

Desserts

Finish with a thick, chocolatey dessert, or corn cakes and syrup. Popular *frangollo* is made of *gofio* and dried fruit doused in syrup. Bananas are readily available, and for dessert are usually served fried or as *bienmesabe* – baked with chocolate and cream.

Malvasia wines on offer at El Patio Museum of Agriculture, Lanzaroto

77F5

✉ 3km from Corralejo

🍴 Small café/kiosk (€) at quayside. Order lunch on arrival or take a picnic and plenty of water with you

🚢 Ferries from Corralejo (➤ 121)

🔄 Corralejo (➤ 80)

ISLA DE LOBOS ✪✪✪

Lying some 3km from Corralejo, the tiny Island of the Seals – as its name literally means – is a haunting miniature world, a curious landscape of tiny volcanic protrusions rising from stones and sand. Was it so named for real seals, as some claim? There are no seals here now. Perhaps instead the *lobos* were the little rock mounds, which from afar do look like animals lying on a beach. The once-volcanic Montaña La Caldera, just 127m high, rises above the rest. Despite being a popular boat outing for tourists, the island has no roads, no vehicles and no inhabitants, and so remains an unspoiled haven of calm and tranquility (➤ 86).

JANDÍA PENINSULA ✪✪✪

In the south, Fuerteventura narrows at the sandy Pared Isthmus, before widening again to form the Jandía Peninsula, originally a separate island. An awesome land of vast skies and beaches, the peninsula is overlooked by Fuerteventura's loftiest peak, the 807m-high extinct Pico de Zarza volcano (also known – you'll understand why as soon as you see it – as Orejas de Asno, 'donkey ears'). All around the steep upland there are long wide swathes of pale sand and immense unspoiled beaches.

76C1

✉ 80km south of Puerto del Rosario

🍴 At Morro del Jable, numerous eateries (€–€€) on the beachside promenade

🚌 No 1 from Puerto del Rosario to Morro Jable via all the resorts and beach stops of the eastern Jandía (six times daily); No 10 is an express service between Morro Jable and Puerto del Rosario via the airport, Caleta de Fuste, Gran Tarajal and Costa Calma; No 5 runs up and down the coast between Costa Calma and Morro del Jable about every hour from 9:30–9:30

🚢 A regular jetfoil service connects Morro Jable with the islands of Gran Canaria and Tenerife

ℹ CC de Jandía, Avenida Saladar, Morro Jable ☎ 928 54 07 76

❷ Local fiestas on the Jandía Peninsula include 16 Jul at Morro del Jable, and the last Sat in Jul at La Pared (➤ 90)

On the peninsula's eastern shore, Playa de Sotavento de Jandía, or simply Sotavento, has 28km of sand. It's the site of the annual World Windsurfing Championships, though what makes this a windsurfer's and kitesurfer's heaven is being protected from the worst of the prevailing winds (Sotavento means 'leeward'). The growing Costa Calma development lies at one end of the windy beach.

South of Sotavento, the coast turns sharply west to the unsightly developments around Jandía Playa resort and to Morro Jable, the peninsula's main town, which has a pleasant promenade, bars and restaurants, and a harbour. Beyond, the extreme tip of the island is edged with beautiful, secluded bays.

On the western side, the broad golden sandy sweep of Playa de Cofete and Playa de Barlovento ('windward') are beautiful but windy, with powerful undercurrents that are dangerous for swimmers. Inland, close to the shacks of Cofete, is the isolated mansion of Herr Gustav Winter, the enigmatic German owner of the whole Jandía Peninsula during and after World War II. Stories abound about Winter (who was given the land by General Franco), his guests and his relations with the German, Spanish and Latin American dictatorships.

The glorious sands at Sotavento Beach at Jandía, a surfer's paradise

85

Isla de Lobos

Distance
10km, plus ferry ride

Time
About 2 hours, plus about 1 hour on the ferry

Start/end point
Corralejo
🔶 77E5

Lunch
Picnic at the lighthouse

Euphorbias are among the few, highly specialised, plants that can live in volcanic terrain

This curious island makes an enjoyable destination for a day out, despite its lack of shade and restaurants. Take a picnic, and be prepared for the breeze and hot, relentless sunshine.

Catch the island ferry from Corralejo at 10. It arrives at about 10:35. On arrival, head off to the right on the main wide track.

At once the track leads through rough terrain of lava and sand. The volcanic rock is streaked and coloured with little plants. On the right is the pretty, rocky Caleta de la Rasca bay, with views towards the dunes of Fuerteventura.

Follow the track through rocky and then sandier terrain. At a succession of little turnings, keep left on the track.

It takes less than an hour to reach the *faro* (lighthouse) at Punta Martiño, at the other end of the island. From here there's a great view back across Lobos and to Fuerteventura and, the other way, to the pale beaches on Lanzarote's southern shore. This is the place to relax with a picnic.

The track now heads towards the middle of the island, with the volcanic Montaña La Caldera rising to the right of the path. At a right turn, walk away from the main track towards the volcano – there are other tracks off to the right and left, but keep heading towards the crater.

After a few minutes' climb you reach the crater edge, from where there's a terrific view of both Fuerteventura and Lanzarote.

Back on the main track, follow it as it curves round to reach the beach near the ferry harbour. Walk on past the beach to get back to the ferry. The boat back to Corralejo leaves at 4, and arrives at about 4:35.

MONUMENTO A DON MIGUEL DE UNAMUNO ✪

At the foot of the volcanic Montaña Quemada, in the hills south of La Oliva, a monument records the exile to Fuerteventura of Miguel de Unamuno (1864–1936), the poet and thinker. While rector of Salamanca University, Spain's most distinguished place of learning, he made no secret of his republican views and openly criticised the monarchy. Banished here in 1924 for his political views, he fell in love with the island's harsh landscapes and lifestyle. After only months, de Unamuno returned to Europe and resumed his cosmopolitan life, yet, in letters and poems he extolled the virtues of Fuerteventura's simple life (➤ 89).

LA OLIVA ✪✪✪

Built in the early 17th century as a residence for Fuerteventura's military governors, this small town was the island's seat of government until 1880. Several fine old mansions survive from those days, though some are now derelict. The grandest of them is the long white La Casa de los Coroneles (the Colonels' House) or La Casa de la Marquesa, dating from 1650 and once belonging to the Cabrera Béthencourt family – their family crest is above the entrance. Opposite is the surprising and enjoyable **Centro de Arte Canario**, which showcases modern art from the islands. Casa de la Cilla, also known as **Museo Grano (Grain Museum)**, is housed in a granary, and has an exhibition on the grains grown on the island.

On the road to Villaverde, windmills are a reminder that this area was a centre for production of *gofio*. North of the town rises sandy 420m-high Montaña Arena.

✚ 77E4
✉ Near the junction of Route 600 (the road to Corralejo via La Oliva) and Route 610 (the road from Puerto del Rosario to Betancuría)
🚍 No 2 (Puerto del Rosario to Vega de Río Palma)
♿ None
↔ La Oliva (➤ 87), Jandía Peninsula (➤ 84–85)

✚ 77E4
✉ 17km south of Corralejo
🍴 Cafés in village (€)
🚍 No 7 (Puerto del Rosario to El Cotillo) stops here three times a day each way Mon–Sat
↔ Monumento a Don Miguel de Unamuno (➤ 87), Corralejo (➤ 80)
❓ Nuestra Señora de la Candelaria, is the big fiesta on 2 Feb

Centro de Arte Canario
☎ 928 86 82 33
🕐 Mon–Sat 10:30–2 Closed Sun
💷 Moderate

Casa de la Cilla, Museo del Grano
☎ 928 86 87 29
🕐 Tue–Sat 10–6
💷 Inexpensive

The splendour of the Casa de los Coroneles has faded over the years, but many charming details – such as the intricate carving around the windows – survive

➕ 77D3
✉ 40km southwest of
Puerto del Rosario
🍴 Bars (€) in the village
🚌 No 4 from Jandía once a
day
♿ None
↔ Ermita de Nuestra Señora
de la Peña (➤ 81),
Tuineje (➤ 89)

PÁJARA ⭐⭐

The parish church of Nuestra Señora de la Regla at Pájara, in the island's western hills, is architecturally one of Fuerteventura's most important historic buildings. Built in sections – a roof beam in the presbytery is marked with the date 1687 – it has an altar that lovers of the baroque will appreciate. The fascinating decorations above the doors on the pink sandstone main porch are much older, and in a style believed to have been inspired by contact with the Aztecs. The village itself is shady and enticing, a rustic farming community in a pleasant fertile setting.

Iglesia de la Virgen, focal point of Pájara's 2 July Fiesta of Our Lady

Did you know ?

Like the French, the Spanish too have their Foreign Legion. Consisting of tough soldiers accustomed to desert conditions, the Spanish Foreign Legion is based on Fuerteventura, at Puerto del Rosario. However, there is little for them to do and rather incongruously they can sometimes be seen on traffic duty.

PARQUE NATURAL DE LAS DUNAS DE CORRALEJO (DUNES OF FUERTEVENTURA, ➤ 18, TOP TEN)

PUERTO DEL ROSARIO ✪

Nothing stood on this spot until the early 19th century, and until as recently as 1956 this unprepossessing town and harbour still went under its original name of Puerto Cabras ('Goat Port'). This seemed rather undignified for a capital city so the grander and prettier name Puerto del Rosario was adopted. It became Fuerteventura's main administrative centre in 1860.

Today the harbour is the most important on the island, and around 50 per cent of Fuertevenura's population live here. Its only visitor attraction is the **Casa Museo Miguel de Unamuno**, devoted to the island's renowned poet exile (➤ 87).

Located beside the main church, this is the house where he lived during his enforced stay in the 1920s. As well as displaying pictures and artefacts about the writer, the house has been faithfully restored.

TEFÍA ✪

At this tiny village, the **Ecomuseo de la Alcogida de Tefía** is a living museum of eight restored traditional houses where you can watch artisans making traditional handicrafts, which include lace, palm baskets and goat's cheese. At nearby Tiscamanita, the **Centro de Interpretación de los Molinos** examines the vital role of windmills in the life of the island.

TUINEJE ✪

At the heart of the island and rather remote, this village – noted for its goat cheese and tomatoes that are grown in fincas all around the town – keeps its ancient Moorish appearance. The altarpiece of the parish church has paintings of the Battle of Tamacita, when locals defeated English pirates. This event is commemorated annually on the 13 October.

Below left: *shell sculpture at Puerto del Rosario's harbour*

✚ 77E4
✉ 30km south of Corralejo
🍴 Café-bars (€) near harbour
🚌 Depot for all bus routes
🚢 Transmediterranean, ☎ 928 85 08 77, operates ferries to Arrecife (Lanzarote), Las Palmas (Gran Canaria) and Santa Cruz (Tenerife)
✈ Flights to and from Arrecife (Lanzaroto) on Binter Canarias ☎ 902 39 13 92, www.binternet.com)
ℹ Avenida Constitución 5 ☎ 928 53 08 44
↔ Caleta de Fustes (➤ 80)
❓ Fiesta de Nuestra Señora del Rosario, 7 Oct

Casa Museo Miguel de Unamuno
✉ Virgen del Rosario 7
☎ 928 86 23 76
🕐 Mon–Fri 9–2
💵 Free

✚ 77E4
Ecomuseo de la Alcogida de Tafía
☎ 928 17 54 34
🕐 Tue–Sat 10–6
💵 Inexpensive
Centro de Interpretación del los Molinos
☎ 928 16 42 75
🕐 Tue–Sat 10–6

✚ 77D2
✉ 32km south of Puerto del Rosario
🚌 No 1 (Puerto del Rosario to Morro Jable)
↔ Gran Tarajal (➤ 81)

Southern Fuerteventura

Distance
120km

Time
4hrs

Start/end point
Morro del Jable
➕ 76C1

Lunch
Simple fish restaurants (€–€€)
in Gran Tarajal and Las
Playitas

This drive explores the wide-open spaces of the Jandía peninsula and the remote, simple towns of the rocky southern interior.

Leave Morro del Jable on the main coast road north (Route 640), passing through Jandía Playa's string of new development at the foot of Jandía's mountain peak, before swinging a few kilometres inland to pass the greatest of Jandía's beaches, Playa de Sotavento (➤ 85). Continue to the left turn for La Pared.

Before the Pared turn, roads on the right lead down to Sotavento beach. Just past the holiday development at Costa Calma, a turn leads into the Istmo de la Pared, the Pared Isthmus. *Pared* means 'wall', and archaeologists believe these dunes marked the division between two Guanche domains – Jandía to the south, and Maxorata to the north. Before that, the Pared dunes did not exist, and the two domains were separate islands.

Las Playitas village, a quiet lunch stop north of Gran Tarajal

Follow the road to La Pared, and stay on it as it turns northward and enters volcanic mountain country. Don't stray off the main road as much of the land is an army firing range. Keep going to Pájara (➤ 88), then follow the road to Tuineje (➤ 89). Join Route 610 to get back to the coast at Gran Tarajal.

Gran Tarajal (➤ 81) is a good place to stop for lunch. Alternatively there is smaller, quieter Las Playitas about 6km further up the coast.

Return inland and turn left onto Route 640 for Tarajalejo. La Lajita is another ex-fishing village growing in popularity. Continue southward along the coast to cross the Pared Isthmus again and return along the coast road to Morro del Jable.

Where To...

Above: *holiday apartments at Morro del Jable, Fuerteventura*
Below: *one of Lanzatore's camels*

Lanzarote

Prices

Approximate price of a three-course meal for one without drinks.

€ = under €15
€€ = €15–€30
€€€ = over €30

Meals with a View

Lanzarote has a number of restaurants with great views, including Castillo de San Jose (➤ 92), Los Cascajos and Mirador de la Valle (both ➤ 95). But for food and drink with an in-flight panorama don't miss Mirador del Río (➤ 95).

Arrecife

Castillo de San José (€€)

Inside the Castillo, attached to the modern art museum, and facing the sea through a panoramic window, this restaurant was designed by César Manrique as a work of art. There are black walls, black tables, and modern classical music playing. The food is sophisticated, well presented, with a moderately priced menu of the day. Can be visited without going to the museum.

✉ Museo Internacional de Arte Contemporaneo, Castillo de San José, Carretera de Puerto Naos (3km north of Arrecife on Muelle de los Mármoles road) ☎ 928 81 23 21 🕐 1PM–3:45PM and 7PM–11PM. Bar 11AM–1AM

Chef Nizar (€€–€€€)

A Lebanese restaurant on Lanzarote may seem unlikely, but it's one of the best places in town for comfortable dining, excellent cooking and friendly service.

✉ Luis Morote 19 ☎ 928 80 12 60 🕐 Lunch, dinner. Closed Sun

Hotel Lancelot (€€)

The restaurant of this pleasant hotel facing Arrecife's sandy beach is open to the public for very reasonable international cooking.

✉ Avenida Mancomunidad 9 ☎ 928 80 50 99 🕐 Lunch, dinner

Leito de Proa (€€)

Choose from mussels, paella, octopus or moray eel at this simple fish restaurant looking out onto the peaceful Charco de San Ginés.

✉ Calle Ribera El Charco ☎ 9928 80 20 66 🕐 9:30AM–midnight

Arrieta

Casa Miguel (€)

This quayside restaurant in a simple little blue and white building at this often-overlooked harbour 7km from Jameos del Agua serves good, unpretentious home cooking.

✉ Calle La Garita ☎ no phone 🕐 Lunch. Closed Mon

Jameos del Agua (€€)

When César Manrique turned this bizarre volcanic feature into a major tourist attraction, he added snack bars and a restaurant serving good Canarian cuisine. There could hardly be a stranger place to eat.

✉ Jameos del Agua, 2km from Arrieta ☎ 928 84 80 24 🕐 Snack bars open 10–6:30; restaurant Tue, Fri, Sat 7PM–1:45AM (folklore show 11PM)

El Lago (€€)

About 10 minutes' walk from the town centre along the shore road, the restaurant has a fine sea view and offers a range of shellfish, fish and meat dishes.

✉ On seafront north of harbour ☎ 928 84 81 76 🕐 Mon–Sat 12–9:30, Sun 12–5

La Caleta de Famara

Las Bajas (€)

Basic, but popular, meat and fish dishes, both international and local, are served at this simple but charming eating place located on the edge of a genuine north coast fishing village.

✉ Avenida Marinero 25 ☎ 928 52 86 17 🕐 9AM–9PM

Casa Ramón (€)

Many visitors pause for a simple unpretentious Spanish lunch of fried fish, paella or pasta at this bar-restaurant beside the road into the village.

✉ **Calle Callejón** ☎ **928 52 85 23** 🕐 **Lunch, dinner. Closed Tue and Jan**

Costa Teguise

Costa Teguise Restaurants

Costa Teguise is divided into three distinct areas for dining purposes: Playa de las Cucharas, in the north of the resort; the busier area around Playa del Jablillo (including Plaza Pueblo Martinero); and the smaller Playa Bastián area at the southern end of town. There is a short drive between each of these districts, and taxis ply between them constantly.

Bar Bastián Restaurant (€€)

Sit on the terrace, order a meal or a drink, and enjoy the sea views from this tourist-oriented beachside brasserie. Open all day long (it serves breakfast as well as lunch and dinner), there's often entertainment such as live music, quizzes and satellite TV for sports fans.

✉ **Avenida del Mar** ☎ **928 59 05 79** 🕐 **9:30AM–midnight**

Casa Blanca (€€)

In a charming little detached building with a hexagonal roof, this unusual grill restaurant in the Jablillo area has a kitchen open to view and dark wooden tables on an enclosed terrace. Local fish dishes and salads are among the choices.

✉ **4 Calle Las Olas** ☎ **928 59 01 55** 🕐 **Dinner**

La Chimenea (€€)

Good Italian food at the main beach. Relaxing decor of cool green and white motif outside, warmer orange and white inside.

✉ **Centro Commercial Las Cucharas** ☎ **928 59 08 37** 🕐 **8:30am–11:30pm. Closed Thu**

Domus Pompel (€€)

Popular and family-run, this place has a very Italian menu of classic dishes well prepared and served in pleasant surroundings.

✉ **Calle Tabaiba 2** ☎ **928 82 71 12** 🕐 **Lunch, dinner**

La Graciosa (€€€)

Gran Meliá Salinas, the smartest hotel on the island, has an elegant restaurant open to the public. Entering on a walkway through tropical gardens and over ponds where goldfish swim adds to the ambience. The food is sophisticated and mainly French, with giant prawns, or sole with scallop mousse. Wonderful desserts. Live music.

✉ **Avenida Islas Canarias** ☎ **928 59 00 40** 🕐 **Dinner. Closed Sun, Mon**

Mesón de la Villa (€€)

An open wood fire is used to cook some of the excellent fish and meat dishes served at this friendly and enjoyable restaurant ideally placed on the waterfront.

✉ **Plaza del Pueblo Marinero** ☎ **928 34 62 71** 🕐 **All day**

Mesón La Jordana (€€€)

One claim to fame here is that Spanish and international celebrities and even royalty have dined at this establishment. Certainly it numbers among Lanzarote's top restaurants, with green and white country-style decor and a

Restaurante Manrique

Several restaurants designed by César Manrique are based on a similar concept: a wide, low structure of sweeping curves, made of volcanic rock, with a panoramic window. But despite the similarities, each is styled to capture the sense of its location. And Manrique thought of every detail. Not only did he personally design the toilets at his sites, but even the rubbish bins were specially adapted for their particular place.

generous, imaginative menu that gives a local flavour to international cooking. Playa Bastían area.

✉ **Calle Los Geranios** ☎ **928 59 03 28** ⏲ **Lunch, dinner. Closed Sun**

Montmartre Bistro (€€€)

A neon 'Moulin Rouge' on the roof is a reminder of the real Montmartre, as are the quarry-tiled floor, oil lamps and pink and white table-cloths. Fine French cooking, with duck liver pâté, and chicken stuffed with prawns served with white wine sauce.

✉ **Avenida de las Palmeras, near corner of Los Calle Geranios** ☎ **928 59 12 05** ⏲ **Dinner. Closed Thu**

Neptuno (€€)

Tucked away in the little plaza at the seafront end of Avenue de Jablillo, this relaxed but stylish bar-restaurant is favoured by well-to-do locals rather than tourists. Concentrating on well-prepared fish and seafood dishes, the cooking has a French/Italian slant, and good Lanzarote wines are served.

✉ **CC Neptuno, Avenida de Jablillo** ☎ **928 59 03 78** ⏲ **Lunch, dinner. Closed Sun**

El Pescador (€€)

Alongside a busy pedestrian plaza, this friendly restaurant invites you to come inside and shut out the noise. Good service and an emphasis on seafood.

✉ **Plaza Pueblo Martinero** ☎ **928 59 08 74** ⏲ **Lunch, dinner**

El Portón (€€)

The friendly staff at this authentic Spanish bar will help you choose from a selection of good-value *tapas* or full meals.

✉ **Calle Las Olas** ☎ **928 59 08 71** ⏲ **Lunch, dinner. Closed Sun**

Villa Mayor (€–€€)

One of the best grill restaurants in the Jablillo area, Villa Mayor has meat and fish freshly cooked to order on the coals at the front of the restaurant. Or sample the homemade pizzas and flambéed desserts.

✉ **Avenida del Jablillo** ☎ **928 59 21 99** ⏲ **Lunch, dinner**

El Golfo

Mar Azul (€–€€)

The terrace of the Azul is right on the water's edge, looking over the Atlantic breakers, and there's an extensive menu of good fresh fish and seafood dishes.

✉ **Avenida Marítima** ☎ **928 17 31 32** ⏲ **Lunch, dinner**

Placido (€€)

Set appealingly right on the beach, this relaxed and likeable family-run restaurant focuses on fresh fish.

✉ **Avenida Marítima 39** ☎ **928 17 33 02** ⏲ **Lunch, dinner**

Guatiza

Jardín de Cactus (€)

Beneath the windmill, big wooden tables under a sail-cloth awning. Enjoy a drink or a light meal and gaze at the amazing cactus garden.

✉ **Jardín de Cactus, Guatiza (17km northeast of Arrecife)** ☎ **928 52 93 97** ⏲ **Daily 10–5:45 (food available until 4)**

Haría

Casal Cura (€€)

One of Lanzarote's best restaurants offering satisfying Canarian food prepared in an atmospheric old house with greenery inside and out. Several local stews like *sancocho*, *puchero* and *potaje* (►82) are served in small intimate dining rooms.

🖂 **Calle Nueva 1 (right turn off road to Yé and Mirador del Rio)** ☎ **928 83 55 56** 🕓 **Lunch, dinner**

Los Cascajos (€)

Just out of town to the north, with great valley views, this rustic restaurant has local speciality dishes and less expensive Spanish favourites. It's also a *bodega*, selling its own wines.

🖂 **Calle María Herera 9** ☎ **928 83 54 71** 🕓 **Lunch Closed Sun**

El Cortijo de Haría (€€)

In an attractive whitewashed converted farmhouse set back from the road, this lively and popular grill restaurant serves classic Lanzarote dishes.

🖂 **Calle El Palmeral 5, on the Teguise road, at the edge of the village** ☎ **928 83 52 65** 🕓 **11–8 (lunch only if reserved)**

Los Helechos (€–€€)

At this big canteen-style restaurant you can feast on the superb view as much as the self-service snacks and light meals.

🖂 **At the viewpoint 5km south of Haría** ☎ **928 83 58 17** 🕓 **10–6**

Mirador de la Valle (€€)

Enjoy a basic snack at this simple viewpoint location looking clear across the Haría valley. Approach slowly – the *mirador* is half-way round a hairpin bend.

🖂 **Los Valles, on the road south of Haría** ☎ **928 52 80 36** 🕓 **Lunch, dinner. Closed Mon**

Mirador del Río (€)

Manrique's starting point when constructing this spectacular site was the bar-restaurant, and the *mirador* is essentially nothing more than a café with a view. Drinks, light snacks, and an exquisite setting.

🖂 **About 7km north of Haría** ☎ **928 52 65 488** 🕓 **Daily 10–5:45**

Isla Graciosa

El Marinero (€)

Visitors to the island can find food and refreshment at this bar-restaurant near the ferry terminal. Fresh fish and local wines are the specialities.

🖂 **Calle García Escámez 14, Caleta del Sebo** ☎ **928 84 20 70** 🕓 **Lunch, dinner**

Volcanic Wines

Other Spanish wines come cheaper, but do try the local wine, red, rosé and white, the latter being especially good. It's made from *malvasia* (or malmsey) grapes, first brought to Lanzarote from Crete in the Middle Ages. Large-scale cultivation of the grape did not begin until after the Timanfaya eruptions of 1730–36: islanders discovered the grapevine was one of the only plants able to thrive in the volcanic dobris. Each bush produces around 200 kilos of grapes per season.

Tapas One

Tapas bars are not a prominent feature of the islands, particularly in the purpose-built modern resorts, but you will find the occasional bona-fide *tapas* bar in the older parts of town and *tapas* (Spanish snacks) are also available in some traditional drinking bars and restaurants. This may be as informal as a few olives, cheese and a wedge of *tortilla* (potato omelette) or it can be a whole variety of dishes which combined make up a substantial meal. Some typical tapas are: *chorizo* (spicy salami-style sausage), *boquerones* (anchovies), octopus salad, prawn salad, Russian salad, *albondigas* (meatballs in a tomato sauce) and the ubiquitous *jamon serrano* (cured mountain ham). The latter either hangs from the ceiling or is placed on the counter in a special cradle-like holder ready for slicing. (► 98)

Mozaga

Casa-Museo del Campesino (€€)

Beside the Campesino Monument and forming part of the museum, this attractive Manrique-built restaurant serves a wide range of traditional Lanzarote dishes, with much use of *gofio*.

✉ **San Bartolomé (on road between San Bartolomé and Mozaga)** ☎ **928 52 01 36** ☻ **Lunch**

Nazaret

Lagomar (€€)

This restaurant is in an extraordinary setting carved into cliffs and connected to the ground by a tunnel and steps, with gardens, caves, a lake and walkways. Choose from imaginative meat, fish and vegetarian dishes, mainly French and Italian in inspiration.

✉ **Calle Loros 6, on the main road between Tahíche and Teguise** ☎ **928 84 56 65** ☻ **Lunch Tue–Sun. Dinner only on Thu, Fri and Sat. Closed Mon**

Orzola

Bahía de Orzola (€)

Blue and white cloths and paintwork mirror the marine location of this popular fish restaurant right on the dockside.

✉ **Calle La Quemadita 1** ☎ **928 84 25 75** ☻ **Lunch, dinner**

Casa Arraez (€)

Rough red painted tables made from old rope spools stand on the quayside at this restaurant, which just looks like a tatty fisherman's shack. Sample the good-value set meal of Canarian stew and dessert, with bread and wine.

✉ **Calle La Quemadita 15** ☎ **928 84 25 86** ☻ **Lunch. Closed Thu**

Punta Fariones (€€)

In a neat blue and white building at the heart of the village beside the little harbour, this modest café-restaurant serves good fresh fish and seafood at reasonable prices.

✉ **Calle La Quemadita 30** ☎ **928 84 25 58** ☻ **All day**

Parque Nacional De Timanfaya

El Diablo (€€)

This broad, low, circular building beside Timanfaya's hottest hot spot is the busy focal point at the summit of the Islote de Hilario. The first of Manrique's landscape architectural works, it has wonderful panoramic views, and good, traditional Canarian cuisine cooked over heat rising directly from the earth.

✉ **Islote de Hilario, Parque Nacional de Timanfaya** ☎ **928 84 00 57** ☻ **Lunch**

Playa Blanca

El Almacén de la Sal (€€)

Right on the waterfront in a converted salt store – the wreck of a rowing boat hangs from the ceiling – this elegant, characterful place has a cool, attractive stone and timber interior. Or sit on the shaded terrace outside, under big parasols. The menu offers the best fresh fish and meat dishes, and many Lanzarote specialities. Live music every evening.

✉ **Paseo Marítimo 12** ☎ **928 51 78 85** ☻ **Lunch, dinner (snacks all day). Closed Tue**

Brisa Marina (€€)
Half-way along the waterside walkway of the old part of the village, this popular place concentrates on tasty fresh fish and seafood. Service can be offhand.
✉ **Avenida Marítima 24** ☎ **928 51 77 92** ⏰ **Lunch**

La Cocina del Mar (€€)
If you can, get a waterside table at this beautifully positioned bar-restaurant near the harbour end of Playa Blanca's promenade. The menu features a wide range of fish, meat and pasta.
✉ **Avenida Marítima 3** ☎ **928 51 86 02** ⏰ **9AM–10:30PM**

Puerto Calero
Amura (€€€)
If you fancy a splurge, this is the place to come. Choose between the minimalist and stylish interior or the waterside outdoor terrace, which has stunning views. The menu is nouvelle cuisine with local and Spanish influences. Dress to impress.
Puerto Calero ☎ **928 51 31 81** ⏰ **Lunch, dinner. Closed Mon**

Puerto del Carmen
La Cañada (€€)
Long-established restaurant just off Avenida de las Playas, serving up delicious local and international dishes. One of the best in town.
✉ **Calle César Manrique 3** ☎ **928 51 21 08** ⏰ **Lunch, dinner. Closed Sun**

Colón (€€€€)
Elegant and tasteful restaurant with ornate tiles and pictures, offering impeccable service. Food is mainly French-style, ranging from fresh fish to the seven-course *menu gastronomique*. Wine buffs will be keen to treat themselves to somethng from the extensive wine list.
✉ **CC Matagorda, Avenida de las Playas 47** ☎ **928 51 59 11** ⏰ **Lunch, dinner**

Especiero (€€)
This enjoyable, good-quality, air-conditioned restaurant with spectacular sea views is a real find. Try one of the speciality flambé dishes or something from the fixed-price menu.
✉ **Avenida de las Playas 46** ☎ **928 51 21 82** ⏰ **Lunch, dinner**

Hannover II (€€)
Located along the busy main strip, this restaurant is especially well liked for its friendly service, good food and generous portions. The paella is recommended.
✉ **Avenida de las Playas 41** ☎ **928 51 02 82** ⏰ **Lunch, dinner**

Lani's Bistro (€€)
Airy, relaxed premises set in a bustling corner location. There is no beach view, but this is a good place to people-watch and enjoy the excellent international range of dishes, desserts and pastries.
✉ **Calle Pedro Barba 10** ☎ **928 51 23 02** ⏰ **9:30AM–11PM**

Lani's Grill (€€)
Good cooking and quick, polite service in several languages. With a rustic wood and ceramic interior, the Grill offers a wide range of meat and fish dishes.
✉ **Avenida de las Playas 5** ☎ **928 51 00 20** ⏰ **6PM–midnight**

Eating out in Puerto del Carmen
There are said to be over 200 restaurants in town, mostly along the Avenida de las Playas. They range from pizzerias to balti to Tex-Mex. Few have any local specialities – Spanish dishes are likely to be gazpacho, paella and other mainland favourites. Restaurants often display photos of the dishes as well as a menu in four or five languages. Few restaurants accept reservations, so stroll along the avenue and chose one which takes your fancy.

Tapas Two

Although *tapas* should not be expensive it's as well to check the price in advance or as you are going along. It's quite easy to spend more on a successsion of snacks than you would on a proper meal. Note too that some kinds of *jamon serrano* are very expensive. Locals sometimes display a curious litter-lout habit of throwing toothpicks, serviettes, sometimes even bits of prawn shell straight onto the floor by the bar. Unless you are a local don't copy them!
(► 96)

Lani's Terraza (€–€€)

Tiled floors, lots of leafy ferns, purple tablecloths and a little bit of mock Roman decor make this a pleasant setting for good, authentic Italian cooking. Tasty hot rolls are served with garlic butter, and a complimentary liqueur.

 Avenida de las Playas 41
☎ 928 51 32 19
🕐 9AM–11:30PM

La Lonja del Fondeadero (€–€€)

In the heart of the old port, this traditional boisterous quayside fried-fish bar has plain wooden tables around a central bar. Excellent fish at low prices, including paella.
✉ Calle Varadero ☎ 928 51 13 77 🕐 All day

Matagorda Park (€–€€)

This unpretentious, authentic Spanish bar-restaurant, also known as Casa Kike, serves excellent grilled meats and freshly caught fish dishes.
✉ CC Matagorda Local 15
☎ 928 51 24 95
🕐 All day

El Molino (€–€€)

Elegant blue-and-white tablecloths and a sprinkling of Spanish specialities make this Pocillos beach restaurant a pleasant change from the rest. Good cooking and service at modest prices.
✉ CC Jameos Playa ☎ 928 51 28 87 🕐 All day

O Bota Fumeiro (€€)

This excellent seafood restaurant on Playa de los Pocillos is Spanish and French rather than Canarian in style.
✉ Alemania 7, CC Costa Luz, Avenida de las Playas
☎ 928 51 15 03 🕐 Lunch, dinner

El Orreo (€€)

Highly professional Galician cooking, attentive service and a great location make this one of the best beachside eateries, with excellent, good-value meat, fish and pasta. Good music.
✉ Avenida de las Playas
☎ 928 51 18 52 🕐 9AM–11PM

Puerto Bahía (€–€€)

Sit at a table overlooking the old port and watching the sun turn the sea red as it sets among the volcanoes. This restaurant on a terrace specialises in fresh fish and seafood.
✉ Avenida de Varadero 5
☎ 928 51 37 93 🕐 All day

Terraza Playa (€€)

Steps decorated with black and white pebbles lead down to a beachside terrace under palm trees. This is a lovely spot, with good food and service, all reasonably priced.
✉ Avenida de las Playas 28
☎ 928 51 54 17 🕐 Lunch, dinner

El Varadero (€€)

Fishing boats pull up along-side this former warehouse, which serves good *tapas*, fresh fish and traditional *papas arrugadas*.
✉ 34 Calle Varadero ☎ 928 51 31 62 🕐 Lunch, dinner

La Santa
Los Charcones (€)

On the main road skirting the village a couple of kilometres from the Club La Santa sports resort, this unpretentious restaurant has a strong Spanish feel, it specialises in local fish and seafood.
✉ Pueblo de la Santa 101, on the Tinajo road ☎ 928 84 03 27
🕐 Lunch, dinner

La Santa (€€)
Popular non-Spanish meat dishes like stroganoff, pepper steak, or *escalope Milanese* dominate a menu geared mainly to residents of nearby Club La Santa sports resort.
✉ **Pueblo de la Santa 14, on the Tinajo road** ☎ **928 84 03 53**
🕐 **Lunch, dinner**

Verde Mar (€)
Encounter the Lanzaroteños on their home ground and get a taste of the fried dishes they love at this basic bar in the village square.
✉ **Plaza Iglesia** ☎ **928 84 08 58** 🕐 **All day**

Teguise
Acatife (€€)
Ambitious and delicious cooking such as cucumber soup with smoked salmon, rabbit in red wine, charcoal-grilled meat, and Lanzarote wines, served in a restored historic building.
✉ **Calle San Miguel 4** ☎ **928 84 50 37** 🕐 **Lunch, dinner. Closed Sun and Mon**

Ikarus (€€)
French-style cooking of fish and meat dishes, plus a good wine list and a romantic bistro atmosphere.
✉ **Plaza del 18 de Julio** ☎ **928 84 53 32** 🕐 **Lunch, dinner. Closed Sun dinner and Mon**

Tías
Casa Tegoyo (€€€)
The elegant and stylish restaurant of this beautiful rural hotel with magnificent views of La Geria serves delicious, imaginative dishes.
✉ **Calle Conil-Asomada 3, Conil (2km from Tías)** ☎ **928 83 43 85** 🕐 **Dinner. Closed Sun and Mon**

Uga
Casa Gregorio (€€)
A traditional Lanzarote inn serving the island's speciality dishes, including fried kid. On Sundays a traditional rich *puchero* stew is served.
✉ **Calle Joaquín Rodríguez 15** ☎ **928 83 01 08**
🕐 **Lunch, dinner. Closed Tue**

Yaiza
La Casona de Yaiza (€€€€)
A former winery, now a beautiful rural hotel and restaurant, the building stands sharply white against the dark volcanic La Geria setting.
✉ **Calle El Rincón 11**
☎ **928 83 62 62**
🕐 **Lunch Mon only, dinner Fri–Wed. Closed Thu**

La Era (€€)
Excellent cooking of local specialities and a good value 3-course set meal are on offer here, in an agreeable old-fashioned atmosphere and delightful setting.
✉ **Carretera General** ☎ **928 83 00 16** 🕐 **Lunch, dinner**

Yé
El Volcán (€€)
This big, cheerful country-style restaurant is situated in the hills near Mirador del Río. Try the great mixed starter of *gofio*, figs, dried fish, sweet potatoes and goat's cheese.
✉ **Plaza de los Remedios** ☎ **928 83 01 56** 🕐 **Daily 8–5. Closed Sat**

Fuerteventura

Wind from Africa

The Sahara sands that cover large areas of Fuerteventura have taken some time to arrive. Although windy on the island, most of the time the air is clear and comes from the north. However, when the sirocco blows – the dry wind from the east – it brings dust as well as heat. The 'dust' is in fact tiny particles of sand. The sirocco blows for short spells at a time, and mainly in winter.

Antigua

La Flor de Antigua (€€)

Eat hearty home cooking, grilled meat and fish, or classic Canarian fare at a spacious and lively eaterie on the Betancuria road.

 Carretera General de Betancuria 43 ☎ **928 87 81 68**
🕐 **Lunch, dinner. Closed Sun**

El Molino (€€)

It feels almost as if you are stepping inside a huge windmill as you enter this round building, which is in fact a beautifully restored former granary. The food is upmarket traditional Canarian cuisine.

✉ **Carretera de Antigua Km 20**
☎ **928 87 85 77** 🕐 **Daily 10–6**

Betancuria

Casa Santa María (€€–€€€)

Opposite the much visited church of Santa Maria, so something of a tourist trap, but still managing to serve enjoyable local food in an atmospheric 16th–century farmhouse.

✉ **Plaza de la Concepcion**
☎ **928 87 82 82** 🕐 **Lunch only**

Don Antonio (€€€)

In a rustic setting south of Betancuría, this appealing bar and restaurant has plenty of local atmosphere and a nice terrace where you can enjoy excellent Canarian cooking.

✉ **Plaza de la Peña, Vega de Rio Palma** ☎ **928 87 87 57**
🕐 **Lunch only, except Sat: lunch, dinner. Closed Mon**

Caleta de Fuste

Mona Lisa (€€)

Good, varied menu of national and international dishes, huge pizzas and salads, and friendly, efficient service. A great place to take the children.

✉ **Ald. Juan Évora Suárez**
☎ **928 16 34 26**
🕐 **Lunch, dinner**

Puerto Castillo (€€)

In a resort full of cheap and cheerful eateries, this harbourside establishment has a better-than-average range of local and inter-national dishes. Excellent fish.

✉ **Harbour** ☎ **928 16 38 77**
🕐 **Lunch, dinner. Closed Sun**

Corralejo

Chablis Wine Bar (€)

Friendly pub-restaurant with all your favourite hearty British dishes – but without the intrusions of TV, karaoke or thumping music. In the centre of town, the Chablis serves breakfast, lunch and dinner in relaxed surroundings. Try the full English breakfast or the roast dinner on Sunday nights.

✉ **Corner Calle Anzuelo and Avenida Franco** ☎ **928 53 52 91**
🕐 **9:30–2, 7– late (no food Sat PM or Wed AM)**

La Marquesina (€€)

Sit at the outdoor tables of this relaxed waterside bar-restaurant close to the small jetty where boats pull up. Fresh fish a speciality.

✉ **Muelle Chico** ☎ **928 53 54 35** 🕐 **All day**

Il Mulino (€€)

Authentic Italian cooking under a wooden arcade in a tiled alley by the harbour. Numerous meat and non-meat sauces to accompany fresh home-made pasta.

✉ **Calle García Escámez 16**
☎ **928 86 71 05**
🕐 **6AM–midnight**

Los Pepes (€€)
Despite a somewhat old-fashioned interior, this restaurant is highly regarded for its excellent food. The chef trained in Switzerland and Germany, worked in some of the UK's finest hotels and the modern international menu with local touches reflects this.

✉ **Calle La Ballena** ☎ **928 53 72 76: www.los-pepes.com** 🕐 **Daily 6:30PM–10:30PM**

Rosie O'Grady's (€)
The best Irish bar in town. Live music every night and home-cooked food.

✉ **Pizarro 10, off Calle de Lepanto, four blocks back from the High Street** ☎ **928 86 75 63** 🕐 **After 7PM**

El Sombrero (€€)
Mock-rustic decor and a touch of style distinguish this good restaurant, specialising in steaks and fondues, on the harbour front. Sit indoors or outside by the water.

✉ **Avenida Marítima 17** ☎ **928 86 75 31** 🕐 **Dinner. Closed Wed**

El Tren (€–€€)
Enjoy fresh fish and seafood dishes at this restaurant in the heart of the town's harbour front area.

✉ **Paseo Marítimo 12** ☎ **928 53 70 93** 🕐 **Lunch, dinner**

Sotavento (€€)
Posters of the different kinds of fish and crustaceans help diners choose from an extensive seafood menu. Chops and steaks are also available. Smaller portions for children

✉ **7 Avenida Marítima** ☎ **928 53 64 17** 🕐 **Lunch, dinner**

Costa Calma
Fuerte Action (€–€€)
Hang out with the local surf dudes and beautiful people at this friendly and relaxed trendy café. Lots of homemade dishes on the menu, including burgers, ice-creams and cakes, also good breakfasts and tapas. There's a terrace outside.

✉ **CC El Palmeral (on main road next to the petrol station)** ☎ **928 87 59 96** 🕐 **Daily 8AM–12.30AM**

Morro Jable/ Playa Jandía
Saavedra (€€)
Go downstairs in the shopping centre to find Spanish atmosphere and Spanish food.

✉ **Avenida Tomás Grau Gurrea, CC Pájara** ☎ **928 16 60 80** 🕐 **Lunch, dinner**

La Pared
Bahía La Pared (€€)
Book a table on the terrace in the early evening at this beachside restaurant to enjoy superb views of the sunset and coastline. There's a children's playground.

✉ **Playa de la Pared** ☎ **928 54 90 30** 🕐 **Lunch, dinner**

Puerto del Rosario
Antiguo (€€€)
One of the island's best restaurants located in Hotel Fuerteventura, but open to the public, the Antiguo offers a reliable menu of Spanish and international flavours.

✉ **Hotel Fuerteventura, Playa Blanca 45** ☎ **928 85 11 50** 🕐 **Lunch, dinner**

Local Information
On Fuerteventura pick up a free copy of the small monthly listings magazine *Grapevine*, which has some useful resort maps, marked with places to eat, drink and be merry. There are also bus and ferry timetables and general information.

Lanzarote

Prices
For a double room, per night in the period Jan–Mar, booked independently, expect to pay:

€ = under €65
€€ = €65–€90
€€€ = over €90

The Manrique Effect
Lanzarote lacks the high-rise hotels of other popular Canary Islands. César Manrique decided on a maximum five floors for hotels in a Zona Turistica (Tourist Zone). Even here, he laid down design guidelines which have been broadly followed. The result is a great success: a seafront not dominated by cheap concrete skyscrapers, but instead with unostentatious white buildings on a human scale, which retain a certain link with the island's culture.

Tour operators featuring Lanzarote offer a wide range of high-quality villas with pools, and less expensive self-catering holiday apartments, as well as the small number of hotels listed here.

Arrecife
Lancelot (€€)
Cool and comfortable, this medium-sized, moderately-priced hotel has a strongly Spanish feel. It faces sandy Playa del Reducto beach, a 5-minute walk from the town centre.
✉ Avenida Mancomunidad 9
☎ 928 80 50 99

Costa Teguise
Beatriz Costa & Spa (€€€)
This hotel is some distance from the sea and the resort's centre. Black, white and red marble in the cool, spacious public areas reflects Lanzarote's colours. Amazing atria have waterfalls, a stream and lush greenery. Outside, a large swimming area has several pools.
✉ Calle Atalaya 3 ☎ 928 59 08 28; www.beatrizhoteles.com

Gran Meliá Salinas (€€€)
This stylish, luxurious hotel overlooks Las Cucharas beach. With a superb cactus garden in front, the hotel encircles wonderful watery tropical gardens inside. Rooms are of the highest standard, with beautiful bathrooms and sea views. Top-quality restaurant.
✉ Avenida Islas Canarias
☎ 928 59 00 40;
www.solmelia.com

Los Zocos Club Resort (€)
Choose between hotel or self-catering accommodation

at this popular family holiday complex 150m from the beach. There's a safe, attractive pool area, restaurants, sports facilties, landscaped grounds and plenty of amusements for all age groups.
✉ Avenida Islas Canarias 15
☎ 928 59 21 22;
www.loszocos.com

Haría
Villa Lola y Juan (€€)
For an away-from-it-all experience, stay at this rural aparthotel, set on a farm and surrounded by fruit orchards and vineyards. Each apartment is furnished in a 1930s style and comes with its own terrace. Outside is an extensive sun terrace and a heated swimming pool.
✉ Calle Fajardo 16 ☎ 928 83 52 56; www.villalolayjuan.com

Playa Blanca
Casa del Embajador (€€€)
This delightful, small family run hotel is in a beachside location. All rooms have views to Fuerteventura and Isla de Lobos. Despite its central position, the hotel is very tranquil. The lack of swimming pool and child-friendly facilties make it more suitable for couples than families.
✉ Calle La Tegala 30 ☎ 928 51 91 91

Timanfaya Palace (€€€)
The spectacular white exterior of domes, turrets, timbers and openings is modelled on traditional local architecture, while a curved frontage à la Manrique arches towards the sea. The lavish interiors are cool, comfortable and stylish. The hotel has a narrow but

pleasant sandy beach in front, lined by a walkway.

✉ **Playa Blanca (Limones end)**
☎ **928 51 76 76**

Puerto del Carmen

Beatriz Playa (€€€)

Adjacent to the beachfront promenade, this comfortable, popular, family-friendly hotel with attractive poolside gardens and terraces is a few paces from shops and restaurants. There is periodic noise from aircraft – the airport lies behind the hotel – but none at night.

✉ **Matagorda** ☎ **928 51 21 66**

Los Fariones (€€€)

One of the island's older hotels, the Fariones stands between Puerto del Carmen's old harbour and its long sandy main beach. A civilised tranquillity pervades the hotel, and the pool area and shaded waterside terraces are delightful.

✉ **Calle Roque del Este 1**
☎ **928 51 01 75**

Los Jameos Playa (€€€)

An impressive, luxurious hotel in the style of a grand Canarian mansion. Wooden galleries surround a central patio with a delightful setting, while the extensive palm-shaded outdoor terrace has swimming pools and an excellent restaurant. There's nightly entertainment – and the dancefloor is reserved for adults after 9PM.

✉ **Playa de los Pocillos**
☎ **928 51 17 17**

Club Hotel Riu Paraíso Lanzarote (€€€)

Hardly visible from the road, this elegant, comfortable low-rise hotel is 30m from Playa de los Pocillos.

Extnsive facilities include seven swimming pools. All inclusive stays only.

✉ **6 Calle Suiza**
☎ **928 51 08 51**

San Antonio (€€)

One of the original hotels on the island, the San Antonio stands in a quiet part of the resort, between Playa de los Pocillos and the main beach. Pleasant palm gardens and heated outdoor pools.

✉ **84 Avenida de las Playas**
☎ **928 51 42 00**

La Santa

Club La Santa (€€€)

Near the village of La Santa on the north shore of the island, this is one of the most highly rated sports resorts in the world. The tremendous range of facilities and full programme of sports and sightseeing activities are reserved exclusively for guests staying at the resort. There are several swimming pools, including a 50m one, four restaurants, a late-night disco, and extensive facilities for young children. Accommodation is in self-catering apartments and must be pre-booked.

✉ **Club La Santa, Tinajo**
☎ **In Lanzarote: 928 59 99 99. In UK: 0161 790 9890**

Yaiza

Finca de los Salinas (€€)

This small inland hotel has plenty of charm. It's cool and peaceful inside, with flagstone floors and a lounge with cane seats arranged around palm trees growing through an open 'ceiling'. Own vegetable gardens and a small farm with animals.

✉ **17 Calle La Cuesta**
☎ **928 83 03 25**

Run for It

Although Club La Santa facilities can only be used by the sport resort's residents, outsiders may enter for the major international prize events held at or organised by Club La Santa, such as the Volcano Triathlon (1.5km swim plus 40km cycle plus 10km run) or the Ironman Triathlon (3.8km swim plus 180km cycle plus 42km run). Prizes can amount to €30,000 or more.

Fuerteventura

Book a Bargain

Most of the hotels listed are available as part of package holidays from tour operators, including return charter flights to the island. Some of the hotels can only be booked through travel agencies, and some only take half-board guests. If you're travelling independently, you'll usually pay more than package tourists – unless you're prepared to make a last-minute call direct to the hotels. Then, any vacant rooms will often be available at low prices.

On Fuerteventura the emphasis is on small-to-medium sized, modern, budget complexes of self-contained chalet-style family accommodation which combine self-catering apartments or chalets with a central reception area and some hotel amenities such as pools, play areas and restaurants. Principal self-catering areas on the island are Caleta de Fustes, Corralejo, Jandía, Playa Barca and the other developments alongside Playa Sotavento.

Caleta de Fustes

Barceló Club El Castillo (€€)

One of many low-rise, inexpensive aparthotel complexes, this member of the Barceló group offers accommodation in one- or two-storey self-catering bungalows with sea views and TV. Facilities include restaurants, bars, a disco, TV room, games room, swimming pools and a childrens' playground. There is evening entertainment.

✉ Caleta de Fustes
☎ From UK: 0845 090 3071; www.barceloclubelcastillo.com

Caleta Amarilla Aparthotel (€)

Located less than 1km from the beach, this plain and simple budget holiday apartment complex with swimming pools offers pleasant chalet-style rooms all with terraces and kitchenettes. Apartments are available on an 'all inclusive' basis.

✉ Caleta de Fustes
☎ 928 16 31 25

Elba Palace Golf (€€€)

This luxurious hotel is built in a traditional Canarian style with wooden balconies and a plant-filled inner patio. Located within the island's only golf club (▶ xx), the hotel features two heated swimming pools, tennis courts, a gym, sauna and jacuzzi.

✉ Urbanización Fuerteventura Golf Club, Carretera de Jandia, Caleta de Fuste ☎ 928 16 39 22

Villas del Castillo (€)

This agreeable complex has 184 self-contained villas in a tropical garden setting with palms and greenery, close to the beach. Each villa is effectively a hotel room with its own kitchenette, TV and terrace. Attractive pool and sunbathing area.

✉ Caleta de Fuste
☎ 928 16 30 44

Corralejo

Los Delfines (€)

This simple, white two-storey complex of small self-catering apartments, each with its own terrace, is attractively arranged around a pool area. The complex has a TV room, supermarket, and a buffet restaurant. Situated on the edge of Corralejo, some 200m from the beach.

✉ Calle El Pozo 3 ☎ 928 53 51 53

Lobos Bahía Club Aparthotel (€€)

An attractive pool complex and bar are at the heart of this better-than-average aparthotel, 800m from the beach. All one and two bedroom apartments have a kitchen area, balcony or terrace, and facilities include bars, restaurants, sports and entertainment programmes. TV room, games rooms, gym, and a small supermarket.

✉ **Calle Gran Canaria 2**
☎ **928 86 71 43**

Club Hotel Riu Oliva Beach Resort (€€€)

A comfortable, well-placed family hotel with small rooms but good access to the vast, beautiful beach, a swimming and sunbathing area, and an all-day children's club. All-inclusive only.

✉ **Avenida Grandes PlayasPlayas (5km south of town)** ☎ **928 86 72 07**

Riu Palace Tres Islas (€€€)

Right on the immense beach that edges the dunes, this stylish, comfortable and well-equipped 365-room hotel is ideally placed for exploring the north of the island. Luxurious bedrooms have private terraces looking over either sea or dunes. Palms and lawns surround a lovely pool and sunbathing area.

✉ **Playas de Corralejo (south of town)** ☎ **928 53 57 01**

Costa Calma
Risco del Gato Suite Hotel (€€€)

One of the pioneers of the south, Risco del Gato is today jostled by its high-rise neighbour but remains unequalled in style and class. Within its landscaped gardens are 51 suites housed in pod-like bungalows, each with a sea view, its own luxury bathroom and private sun terrace. A spa, gym and gourmet restaurant looks after its mainly Spanish and German well-heeled clientele.

✉ **Calle Sicasumbre 2**
☎ **928 54 71 75,**
www.hotelriscodelgato.com

Jandía
Sol Gorriones Sol (€€–€€€)

Recently renovated hotel in a beautiful, isolated position right on Sotavento beach with pools, sun terraces and gardens. Excellent facilities include a health centre, gym, tennis courts and the famous Rene Egli windsurfing school.

✉ **Playa Barca, Costa Calma**
☎ **928 54 70 00**

Iberostar Palace (€€€)

Located on a 25km-long stretch of beach, this 437-room four-star hotel is 1km from Jandía. It has an extensive pool complex that includes a jacuzzi and children's and heated pools, bars, restaurants, a dive centre and an entertainment programme.

✉ **Los Gaviotas**
☎ **928 54 04 44**

Sol Jandía Mar Apartments (€)

Dark hills and a golden beach provide the setting for this pleasant 294-apartment complex with two swimming pools, restaurant, bars, sports facilities and play areas. There's nightly entertainment and a disco, and more entertainment and facilities in the centre of the resort, about 10 minutes' walk away.

✉ **Avenida Jandía, Morro Jable** ☎ **928 54 13 25**

Pájara
Hotel Rural Casa Isaítas (€€)

Housed in a stone building dating from 1890, this is a charming, friendly hotel with just four rooms, all furnished in an attractive rural style, a library and a great restaurant.

✉ **Calle Guize 7** ☎ **928 16 14 02; www.casaisaitas.com**

Home from Home

Both Lanzarote and Fuerteventura have placed great emphasis on villa holidays as a way of spreading tourists across a wider area, providing them with unobtrusive accommodation in the local style, and enabling them to contribute more to the economy.

Markets

African Traders
Colourfully dressed Africans in the market squares of Lanzarote and Fuerteventura bring an exotic note to the Spanish scene. These West African trading families, often Senegalese, make the boat trip specifically to sell in European markets, and stay for several months. Usually the whole family sits at different stalls selling very similar goods, or women may sit together grooming each other, breast-feeding, while older children tap idly at African drums.

Almost every town has its weekly or even daily market. These rarely have any of the fruit, vegetables or live chickens of traditional country markets. Stallholders are usually Africans selling African handmade goods; northern Europeans selling their own craftwork; and Spanish market traders selling linens, embroidery, lace, cloth goods or ceramics.

African Craftwork
Items for sale will include carved wooden masks, wooden toys, studded or tooled leatherwork and authentic African drums. In addition there are historic tribal artefacts, such as ancient ceremonial masks, which should perhaps not have found their way into the market. Nothing has a marked price. Don't buy ivory goods (illegal in the European Union) or cheap European and Far Eastern imitations.

Local Lace, Crochet and Embroidery
The most common items are tablecloths, placemats, napkins, bedlinen and handkerchiefs. These are by no means always cheap, but are good value for such high-quality handmade work, and have distinctively Spanish designs and character.

Ceramics
Tiles, glazed pottery and attractively handpainted crockery make excellent gifts or souvenirs but can be heavy and fragile for air-travellers. However, small items, well-packed, make a distinctive and worthwhile purchase.

Crafts
As well as the fine cloth goods, you'll also see good costume jewellery (often including peridot, the translucent semi-precious volcanic stone), basketware, straw hats, and unusual local pottery, traditionally made without a potters' wheel. Handicrafts with delicate woodwork includes the *timple*, the tiny Canarian stringed instrument that originated at Teguise.

Teguise
The main shopping event is the large Sunday market in Teguise, which operates from 9AM to 2PM. A vast array of stalls is crammed into almost every inch of the little town. Tourists are brought by special buses from resorts all around the island, and countless others come in by rented car or even on foot, until Teguise is bursting with the crowd. The carnival-like atmosphere is often enhanced by colourful folklore shows and traditional events.

Other Markets
Arrecife
Saturday morning at El Charco de San Ginés.

Costa Teguise
Friday from 6PM onwards in Plaza Pueblo Marinero.

Playa Blanca
Wednesday morning in Punta Limones shopping centre.

Mancha Blanca
During the Virgen de los Volcanes pilgrimage to Mancha Blanca peak in mid-September there is a big street market of traders from all of the Canary Islands.

Duty Free Shopping & Souvenirs

Duty Free

The Canary Islands have a long history as a Duty Free zone. Even though – as part of Spain – they are now in the EU, the islands continue to have exemption from certain taxes and duties on goods imported from outside the EU.

In the main towns, especially tourist resorts, dozens of shops offer electronic goods, cameras, binoculars and other optical equipment, CD and DVD players, perfumes and other luxury items at discount prices. Prices are similar to those in airport shops and other duty-free outlets. Alcohol of all types is generally especially good value.

Beware though, do not simply assume 'tax free' prices are a bargain: many tourists discover too late that they have paid almost as much (and sometimes more) than the usual shop price. Most of the shop-keepers are Indian and are accustomed to haggling over prices.

Be especially on your guard against counterfeit or defective items, and watches or similar goods with fake designer names. Bona fide electronic goods should be accompanied by proper international warranties and service details.

In Lanzarote, you'll find several shops along Avenida de las Playa in Puerto del Carmen. In Fuerteventura head for Calle Gen Franco in Corralejo.

Manrique Designs

Fundacíon César Manrique Shops
T-shirts and other clothes with Manrique logos and designs, jewellery and other goods to his design, and prints of his work are available at Fundación César Manrique shops:

✉ **Main shop: Casa-Museo Fundación César Manrique, Taro de Tahíche.**
Other shops: 26 José Betancort, Arrecife; 10 Diaz Otilía, Arrecife. Arrecife airport.
La Lonja, Playa Blanca.
Avenida Papagayo 6, Playa Blanca.
Tourist office, Avenida de las Playas, Puerto del Carmen.
La Lonja, Teguise
Calle Plaza del 18 de Julio 6, Teguise

Flowers that Fly
Exotic, Canary-grown strelitzias – bird-of-paradise flowers – are widely available and make a popular, impressive gift. They should be ordered in advance and picked up on the day of your departure. They come specially wrapped and packaged for air travel. Alternatively, they can be bought in the departure lounge at Arrecife airport.

Edible Souvenirs
Interesting presents or tasty reminders of your stay include *mojo* sauces (▶ 82), available in small gift packs, and local wine, which can be chosen and sampled in the *bodegas* of Lanzarote's Geria Valley (▶ 26).

Children's Activities

Children Welcome
The islanders, like other Spaniards, never make kids feel excluded. It's a sign, perhaps, of their affection for children, that restaurants, bars and cafés don't generally list children's menus and children's portions. Instead, children are warmly welcomed, indulged, given little portions, and allowed in to any establishment at any hour of day or night.

Family Beaches

Lanzarote

Caleton Blanca
Warm and sheltered. The swimming is safe here and there are rock pools to explore.
✉ **1km south of Orzola**

Papagayo
Four connected beaches considered to be the best on the island (➤ 50–51).
✉ **6km east of Playa Blanca**

Playa Dorada
A lovely curve of golden sand in a sheltered bay.
✉ **Playa Blanca**

Playa Grande
Sandy, fun and a good base for water sports (➤ 65).
✉ **Puerto del Carmen**

Playa de los Pocillos
A huge sweep of sand. The Jameos end has child-friendly snackbars and restaurants.
✉ **Puerto del Carmen**

Fuerteventura

Corralejo Dunes
Superb dunes within reach of civilisation (➤ 18).
✉ **Corralejo**

Sotavento Beach
Long expanse of glorious sand. More sheltered than many beaches on this windy island (➤ 85).
✉ **Jandía Peninsula**

Other Attractions

Many of the sights thrill kids every bit as much as grown-ups. The sights most likely to appeal to the younger generation are listed here.

Lanzarote

Arrieta
Cueva de los Verdes
The haunting music and lighting make a visit to this fascinating cave system a magical experience (➤ 17).
☎ **928 17 32 20** ⏰ **Regular tours daily 10–5**

Jameos del Agua
Spotting the tiny blind white crabs, the amazing auditorium in a cave, and – most of all – the Casa de los Volcanes hands-on science museum at the top of the cliff will amuse any child (➤ 22).
☎ **928 84 80 20** ⏰ **Daily 10–6:30**

Costa Teguise
Aqua Park
This water park has fantastic waterslides and flumes, lovely swimming pools and sunloungers and shaded areas for the grown-ups.
✉ **2km inland from Costa Teguise** ☎ **928 59 21 28** ⏰ **Daily 10–6** 💷 **Expensive**

Guatiza
Jardín de Cactus
Is that cactus real? Especially the giant cactus outside? Go and see. One thing is for certain, the 1,400 varieties inside the garden are genuine and very weird (➤ 23).
✉ **Just outside Guatiza** ☎ **928 52 93 97** ⏰ **Daily 10–6**

Guinate
Parque Tropical
Little ones will enjoy this bird world in northern Lanzarote, where some 300 species of birds can be seen (➤ 62) and there are regular shows by performing parrots.
✉ **Guinate (4km from Haría)** ☎ **928 83 55 00** ⏰ **Daily 10–5**

Puerto del Carmen

Blue Delfin

Variety of trips and mini-cruises daily in a glass-bottomed catamaran, plus free bus transfers. If fully booked there are several similar companies.

☎ 928 51 23 23

Gran Karting Club

Lanzarote's premier go-karting track. Karts come in all sizes to suit adults as well as children. The site also has a bar, cafeteria and playground.

✉ La Rinconada, Arrecife road
☎ 619 75 99 46;
www.grankarting.com
🕐 Daily 10–9

Submarine Safaris & Tours

Journey in a real submarine, with high-tech viewing.

✉ Puerto Calero
☎ 928 51 28 98

Taro de Tahíche

Fundación César Manrique

Children will be entranced by the house Manrique made for himself, especially the underground rooms in sphe-rical lava bubbles (➤ 19). The adults will be fascinated too.

☎ 928 84 31 38 🕐 Mon–Sat 10–6

Manrique Mobiles

Manrique's mischievous inventiveness strikes a chord with the youngest art-lovers when they see his mad mobiles, standing at junctions and roundabouts like giant coloured toys turning, whirling and whizzing in the wind. See if you can spot the one at the airport as soon as you arrive in Lanzarote.

Timanfaya

Islote de Hilario

Only the youngest or weariest of children could fail to be astonished by the fire and water magic at the hottest spot on the volcanic island (➤ 20–21).

Yaiza

Camel Rides

Not for everyone, but unlike with other camel rides, on these you don't sit on the camel but in seats on the animal's side. Rides are based at the Camel Park below Timanfaya (➤ 58).

Fuerteventura

Corralejo

Carnival

A dazzling show which allows wild behaviour. Failing that, enjoy the crazy noise, colour and flamboyance of any local fiesta.

🕐 Feb or Mar

Catamarán Celia Cruz

Glass-bottomed catamaran boat trips to Lobos Island.

☎ 646 53 10 68 🕐 Departs daily at 9:45AM, returning at 2.20PM and 5PM

Lajita

La Lajita Oasis Park

The main attraction of this zoo is a 30-minute ride on one of its herd of 250 dromedaries. Ponies and donkeys are also available for rides. As well as various shows – sea lions, birds of prey or crocodiles – there are hundreds of species of birds, primates and mammals. Recent additions include giraffes and rhinoceroses.

✉ Carretera General de Jandía, FV-2 Km 57.4 ☎ 928 16 11 35 🕐 Daily 9–7

Late Nights

Your children will be quick to notice one Spanish custom they'll want to follow on holiday: there is no bedtime. Spanish families can often be seen out as late as midnight, having dinner or going for a stroll together. Restaurants think nothing of catering for children in the evening. Even at home, children are often up playing while the grown-ups talk until late. It's taken for granted that children are a constant part of family life.

Sports – On Water

Wind (for Windsurfers)
It is the regular, strong north-by-northwest trade wind (known as Los Alisios and often reaching force 4 or 5) blowing in from the Atlantic that makes Lanzarote and Fuerteventura such an excellent centre for windsurfing. The winds don't always blow, however: the average reliability rate is around 50 per cent in winter and 60–75 per cent in summer. The western, windward coasts can offer thrilling sport for experienced windsurfers, but beware – El Cotillo beach on Fuerteventura is said to break more kit than any other surf location in Europe!

Big Game Fishing

Hunting for shark, barracuda, swordfish, marlin, tuna, wahoo, dorado and the other big Atlantic fish is popular on both islands. Hire a boat or join an excursion.

Lanzarote

Puerto Calero
Catlanza
Daily deep sea fishing excursions by catamaran. Yachts and motorboats for private hire.
✉ **Puerto Calero** ☎ **928 51 30 22**

Fuerteventura

Corrajelo
Pez Velero
Daily excursions in 33ft catamaran fishing for barracuda, tuna, bluefish and bass.
✉ **Casa Mar y Juan, Pesca Deportiva, Calle Caravela 6** ☎ **928 86 61 73**

Diving & Scuba Diving

Good underwater visibility in a climate where diving is possible year round, has made this a favourite sport on the two islands. The underwater lava has created many reefs, caves and unusual rock formations. There is an abundance of wildlife, including sharks, eels, octopus and rays, as well as big fish, sponges, anenomes, crustaceans and colourful coral.

Lanzarote

Costa Teguise
Calipso Diving
Top quality diving and scuba diving for all levels (minimum age 12).
✉ **Centro Comercial Nautical, Local 3, Avenida Islas Canarias** ☎ **928 59 08 79**

Diving Lanzarote
High-quality scuba diving centre on Las Cucharas Beach, with variety of hire and excursion options, including night diving.
✉ **Playa de las Cucharas** ☎ **928 59 04 07**

Playa Blanca
Cala Blanca Diving Centre
PADI courses. Guided dives and equipment hire.
✉ **CC El Papagayo 66** ☎ **928 51 90 40**

Puerto del Carmen
Atlantica Diving Center
Diving courses from the main beach.
✉ **Aparthotel Fariones Playa, Calle Acatife 2** ☎ **928 51 07 17**

RC Diving Delfin Club
Try-out lessons, training courses and organised dives.
✉ **CC Aquarium, 38 Avenida de las Playas 38** ☎ **928 51 42 90**

Safari Diving
This PADI five-star, highly professional centre for diving includes instruction and welcomes divers of all qualifications, as well as divers with disabilities, beginners, non-divers, and children, for a wide range of courses. Organised dives include night diving.
✉ **Playa de la Barrilla** ☎ **928 51 19 92**

Fuerteventura

Corralejo
Dive Center Corralejo
Enjoy a whole day's dive with instructor, including audio-visual training. If you are an experienced diver with certification and logbook, the Dive Center offers boat dives daily (except Sun) at 8:30AM and 10:30AM in different locations. PADI courses also available.
✉ **Calle Nuestra Señora del Pino 22** ☎ **928 53 59 06;**
www.divecentercorralejo.com

Surfing
Fantastic wind and waves make these islands great for surfers.

Fuerteventura

Corralejo
Ineika Funcenter
A range of courses of one or two weeks, fully inclusive of equipment, transfers and breakfast. Other equipment, such as boards and wetsuits, available for rent.
✉ **Ineika Apartamentos 53**
☎ **928 53 57 44; .**
www.ineika.de

Natural Surf
Instruction courses and equipment hire.
✉ **Calle Acorazado España 10**
☎ **928 53 57 06**

Ventura Surf
Instruction courses and equipment hire
✉ **Maya de la Galera** ☎ **928 86 62 95**

Windsurfing and Kitesurfing
This is by far the most popular sport in the Canary Islands. Every main resort beach in Lanzarote and Fuerteventura has facilities for windsurfing rentals and instruction. Fuerteventura is considered one of the world's best locations for windsurfing, and Jandía's Playa de Sotavento is the site of the annual World Windsurfing Championships mid-July to mid-August.

Lanzarote

Costa Teguise
Windsurfing Club Nathalie Simon
Courses and equipment hire at this windsurfing centre at Playa Las Cucharas. Canoes also for rent.
✉ **CC Puerto Tahíche, Local 18, Calle Las Olas**
☎ **928 59 07 31;**
www.sportaway-lanzarote.com

Fuerteventura

Corralejo
Flag Beach Windsurf and Kitesurg Centre
Windsurfing, kitesurfing and surfing tuition and equipment rental. Packages including accommodation, airport transfers and car hire.
✉ **General Linares 31** ☎ **928 86 63 89**

Ventura Surf
Tuition and rentals from one hour to 14 days.
✉ **8 Hoplaco Aptos** ☎ **928 86 62 95**

Playa Barca
Center René Egli
The Jandía peninsula's principal windsurfing base, with tuition and rentals, right on Sotavento beach.
✉ **Sol Hotel Los Gorriones**
☎ **928 54 74 83**

Wind (for Holidaymakers)
The north-by-northwest trade wind brings stable, rain-free days with some cloud. On the north or west of the islands, the wind can be troublesome, and the cloud cover excessive. In the south and east, it means perfect holiday weather. The occasional alternatives are the moist southerly winds or the unpleasant, warm dry sirocco that blows sand over from the Sahara.

Sports – On Land

Grin and Bare It
Topless sunbathing is acceptable on all beaches, especially the main beaches of Puerto del Carmen, Costa Teguise, Playa Blanca, Corralejo and Jandía. Naturism, or stripping off completely, is not acceptable on resort beaches, but common on any secluded stretch of coast, or beaches outside resorts, such as Playa Papagayo on Lanzarote, or, on Fuerteventura, the Corralejo beach away from the hotels.

Aerial Sports

Lanzarote

Paragliding, Hang-gliding, Skyjumping
These are all keenly practised on Lanzarote – by experts. Unpredicatable winds (strong at higher altitudes) increase the thrill for the most experienced, but make the sports off-limits for beginners. The most popular spots, especially for hang-gliders, are the soaring sea cliffs at Famara in the north of the island. It's best to bring your own equipment.

Cycling

Thanks to the dry weather and lack of traffic, cycle touring is fun on these islands. Choose between easy-going flatter terrain near the resorts, and more challenging hills inland. Wherever you go take plenty of drinking water.

Lanzarote

Arrecife
Ciclomania
Rental of mountain bikes for all ages. Children´s seats also available.
✉ **Calle Almirante Boado Endeiza 9 (opposite the Gran Hotel)** ☎ 928 81 75 35

Costa Teguise
Bike Station
Good quality bikes with extras at no additional cost.
✉ **CC Maretas (near post office)** ☎ 628 10 21 77

Tommy's Bikes
The leading and longest established hire shop for top-quality touring, racing and mountain bikes. This friendly, helpful company gives free advice and maps, and recommends and organises island tours and excursions. A typical excursion lasts a whole day, including jeep transfers, bikes, water, tour guide, boat transfers where necessary.
✉ **Galeón Playa (on the harbour near Playa del Jablillo)** ☎ 928 59 23 27

Fuerteventura

Corralejo
Vulcano Biking
Touring cycles and mountain bikes for hire.
✉ **10 Calle Acorazado España** ☎ 928 53 57 06

Golf

Lanzarote

Costa Teguise
Club de Golf de Costa Teguise
Lanzarote's only golf course is considered one of Europe's most unusual and exciting places to play. The tender green turf of the 18-hole, 72-par course looks dazzling amid the dark hills, cacti and palms. No handicap is required. The course offers a driving range, putting and pitching greens, buggy, trolley and club hire, and a club house with bar-restaurant, lounge and pro-shop. Lessons are available.
✉ **2km up Avenida del Golf** ☎ 928 59 05 12

Horse Riding

Lanzarote

Puerto del Carmen
Rancho Texas Lanzarote
This western theme park

offers pony rides as well as falconry displays, animal enclosures and country and western evenings. Self-catering bungalows for rent. There is a children´s adventure playground and restaurant on site.

✉ **Calle Noruega (signposted from Playa de los Pocillos beach)** ☎ **928 17 32 47; www.ranchotexaslanzarote.com**

Uga
Lanzarote a Caballo (Lanzarote on Horseback)
Horse riding in the Geria Valley, Playa Quemada or Playa Blanca as well as camel rides and paintball combat.

✉ **On Arrecife–Yaiza road, close to Uga** ☎ **928 83 00 38**

Fuerteventura

Finca Crines del Viento
In Triquivijate near Antigua are these stables, with horse riding for beginners and experienced riders. English and German spoken.

☎ **928 17 46 00/609 00 11 41**

Motorbiking
A motorbike is a good way to explore the spectacular terrain. (► panel)

Sports Centres

Lanzarote

Puerto del Carmen
Centro Deportivo Fariones
Located opposite Fariones Hotel, this sports centre has a heated swimming pool, gym, sauna, jacuzzi, tennis and squash courts.

✉ **Calle Roque del Este 1**
☎ **928 51 47 90**

Walking
There are numerous possible routes on both islands, but note that walking on the volcanic *malpaís* is difficult and uncomfortable. Don't set off on your own, and take adequate supplies (of drinking water, high-energy food and protective gear) with you on longer trips. Wear sturdy footwear.

Lanzarote

Timanfaya
Canary Trekking
Guided volcano walks, including a visit inside a lava tunnel.

☎ **609 537 684; www.canarytrekking.com**

ICONA National Parks Walking Service
Two guided walks in Timanfaya National Park , to a volcano or along the coast. The volcano walk, the Tremesana Route (► 56) is the easier of the two. Groups are small and the emphasis is on the geology of the *malpaís* and its native species.

✉ **Mancha Blanca Interpretation Centre** ☎ **928 84 08 39**

Fuerteventura

Villaverde
Hannelore von der Twer
Guided walks in many areas including Monte Arena.

✉ **Villa Volcana**
☎ **928 86 86 90 or 608 92 83 80**

Motorbiking
The open roads and lack of traffic make the islands attractive places for biking. A few words of warning, however. If you intend going offroad make sure you have a sufficiently powerful machine not to get bogged down in sand, particularly if you have a pillion rider or much luggage. Beware too that lava tracks are extremely bumpy. Fill up with petrol on Saturdays, as on Sundays many petrol stations only have automatic pumps working. The smallest note they accept is €10, which will buy far more fuel that you need if you only have a small petrol tank. The free island map from tourist offices usefully shows all petrol stations. And, finally, the cost of hiring a bike may not be any cheaper than a car – shop around as much as you can.

Gastronomy & Nightlife

The Wine-grower's Art
In 1964–65 the region around La Geria, Lanzarote's main wine-producing area, was dubbed 'Engineering without Engineers' by the Metropolitan Museum of Modern Art in New York because of its ingenious 'vineyards'. The largest *bodega* on the island, El Grifo, now exports its wines all over Europe.

Gastronomy

Lanzarote

La Geria
Bodegas Barreto
Free wine tasting at this Lanzarote wine cellar.
✉ At El Campesino, on La Geria road ☎ 928 52 07 17
🕐 Daily 10–6:30

Mozaga
Bodegas Mozaga
Wine tasting and wine buying at this popular producer of Lanzarote wines.
✉ On Arrecife–Tinajo road
☎ 928 52 04 85 🕐 Daily 8:30AM–6PM

San Bartolomé
El Grifo Bodega and Museo del Vino
The oldest working *bodega* on Lanzarote. Take a look at the old winepress and 18th-century wine-making equipment, have a half-hour guided stroll in the vineyards and enjoy the wine tasting. A sculpture of a griffin by César Manrique stands at the entrance to the *bodega*.
✉ On road to Uga ☎ 928 52 40 12; www.elgrifo.com
🕐 Bodega daily 10–4, Museo daily 10:30–6

Uga
El Faro
Tasting of Lanzarote's salty, traditionally made goat's cheeses.
✉ On Teguise–Uga road
☎ 928 17 31 13

Casinos

Lanzarote

Puerto del Carmen
Casino de Lanzarote
Slot machines, blackjack and roulette tables, as well as restaurant, bar and entertainment. Admittance is for over-18s only – and you will need your passport as proof of age. However, there is a terrace with a bar where all ages are allowed.
✉ Avenida de las Playas 12
☎ 928 51 50 00 🕐 Slot machines: 11AM–4AM. Bar and game hall: 5PM–4AM. Bar and terrace: 9AM–4AM. Restaurant: 9PM–2AM

Discos and Late-night Bars

All the resorts on both islands have late-night bars with music, but there are few real discos or dance venues. Those listed here open around 9 or 10PM (although they only really start filling up about midnight) and stay open until 2 or 4AM.

Lanzarote
Avenida de las Playas in Puerto del Carmen is Lanzarote's 'entertainment hub', with a large number of late-night bars featuring live music and dancing. The focal point for most of the city's discos and nightclubs is the Centro Atlántico block, situated on the Avenida about half-way along the main beach. Popular nightclubs here include the Big Apple and Cesars.There is also the relatively low-key Casino de Lanzarote (see earlier entry). In Arrecife, head to Calle José Antonio for the best nightlife.

Arrieta
Jameos del Agua
After dark on Tuesday, Friday and Saturday, these water caverns in the north of the

island become a popular nightclub, where crowds drink, dine and dance in the extraordinary underground setting.

✉ **Near Arrieta, 26km north of Arrecife** ☎ **928 84 80 20**
🕐 **Tue, Fri & Sat 7PM–1:45AM. Folklore show 11PM**

Costa Teguise
Baobab Club
A popular club that plays a variety of music.

✉ **2nd floor, Centro Teguise Playa (Jablillo area)**

Puerto del Carmen
Big Apple
Smallish dance floor; more upmarket feel. Outdoor seating for when it gets hot.

✉ **Centro Atlantico**

Cesars
Nightclub with big dance floor and lively atmosphere.

✉ **Centro Atlantico**

Fuerteventura

Caleta de Fustes
Cavern
Bar with mostly 60s music; attracts both young and older folk.

✉ **The Harbour**

Corralejo
Blue Rock
Small bar playing rock and blues music with outdoor terrace.

✉ **Just off the front, to the right of the tourist office**

Rock Island
Friendly bar featuring regular live acoustic music. Also has an extensive cocktail list.

✉ **Calle Crucero Baleares 8**
☎ **928 53 53 46** 🕐 **from 7:30PM**

Hotels
Many hotels offer cabaret, dancing, karaoke or musicians, most evenings from about 10PM until midnight. There's no need to be a guest at the hotel. Check the weekly programme displayed at hotels.

Lanzarote

Costa Teguise
Melia Salinas Hotel
✉ **Avenida Islas Canarias**

Playa Blanca
Timanfaya Palace Hotel
✉ **West of the harbour**

Puerto del Carmen
Los Fariones Hotel
✉ **Harbour end of main beach**

Fuerteventura

Corralejo
Riu Palace Tres Islas
✉ **Playas de Corralejo**

Canarian Wrestling
A favourite spectator sport for the islanders is their traditional wrestling (*Lucha Canaria*), for which the combatants wear a particular style of shorts and shirt. Wrestlers work in teams, whose members are pitted against each other one-to-one, in turns. The fight involves holding onto the side of your opponent's shorts and attempting to throw him to the ground. It's slow and cautious, with long waits for sudden moves. Contests are staged from time to time, and your hotel or the tourist office should have details of forthcoming matches. This 'clean' sport is very fair and totally different from European wrestling. It provides great family entertainment. Tourists are made welcome, and this is a good way to meet the locals.

What's On When

Carnival Islands

Carnaval brings two weeks of music, dancing, noise, parades, craziness and energy, which on Lanzarote is held mainly on the waterside promenades of Arrecife and Puerto del Carmen. It ends on Ash Wednesday with the zany ceremony of the Burial of the Sardine. For this farcical finale, black-clad mourners sob as a tiny coffin containing the sardine is buried on the seashore. The festival may be less grandiose on Fuerteventura, but has the advantage of being held at several places all over the island. Small towns and villages will put on their own days of colourful, enthusiastic parades and processions, including a day devoted to the Childrens' Carnival.

January

Cabalgata de los Reyes Magos Festival (Three Kings Parade, 5 Jan): Teguise.

February

Fiesta de Nuestra Señora de Candelaria (Candlemas, 2 Feb): a big festival and pilgrimage in certain villages, for example Gran Tarajal and La Oliva on Fuerteventura.
Carnaval (two weeks, dates vary each year: 20 Feb 2007, 5 Feb 2008): especially exuberant in Arrecife on Lanzarote, and Corralejo on Fuerteventura (► panel).

March/April

Easter: look out for big events all over the islands during Easter Week.

May

Fiestas on Fuerteventura include: Tarajalejo (8 May) La Lajita (13 May).

June

Fiesta de San Juan (24 Jun): celebrating the midsummer, Haría, Lanzarote.
Corpus Christi: Arrecife and Haría, Lanzarote. Patterns of sea salt decorate the ground.

July

Fiesta de Nuestra Señora de Regla (2 Jul): Pájara, Fuerteventura.
Fiesta de San Buenaventura (14 Jul): Betancuría, Fuerteventura, festival to honour the town's patron saint and the incorporation of the island into Spain.
Fiesta de Nuestra Señora del Carmen (16 Jul): Teguise, La Graciosa, Arrecife and Puerto del Carmen, Lanzarote; Corralejo, Morro Jable, Fuerteventura.
Fiesta (last Sat in Jul): La Pared, Fuerteventura. On the last Saturday fishing boats put out to sea with effigies of the saint aboard.

August

Fiesta de San Ginés (whole month): everywhere, but especially Arrecife, Lanzarote. Processions, parades and traditional dancing in the streets.
Semana de la Juventud (Youth Week, from mid-Aug onwards): Gran Tarajal, Fuerteventura.

September

Fiesta de Nuestra Señora de Antigua (8 Sep): in honour of Antigua's patron saint, Fuerteventura.
Fiesta de Nuestra Señora de Guadalupe (8 Sep): Teguise, Lanzarote .
Virgen de los Volcanes (15 Sep): general pilgrimage (*romería*) to Mancha Blanca, Lanzarote. The highlight is a re-enactment of the Virgin, the patron saint of Lanzarote, stopping the lava flow.
Fiesta de Nuestra Señora de la Peña (3rd Sat): Vega del Río Palmas, Fuerteventura.
Fiesta de San Miguel (29 Sep): Tuineje, Fuerteventura.

October

Fiesta de Nuestra Señora del Rosario (7 Oct): Puerto del Rosario, Fuerteventura.
Battle of Tamacita (13 Oct): Tuineje, Fuerteventura.

November

Fiesta de San Diego de Alcalá (13 Nov): Gran Tarajal, Fuerteventura.

December

Christmas: nativity plays and processions take place all over the islands.

Practical Matters

Above: *the road to Sóo, Lanzarote*
Right: *shell sculpture in the harbour at Puerto del Rosario, Fuerteventura*

TIME DIFFERENCES

GMT 12 noon	Canaries 12 noon	Germany 1PM	USA (NY) 7AM	Netherlands 1PM	Spain 1PM

BEFORE YOU GO

WHAT YOU NEED

● Required
○ Suggested
▲ Not required

Some countries require a passport to remain valid for a minimum period (usually at least six months) beyond the date of entry – contact their consulate or embassy or your travel agent for details.

	UK	Germany	USA	Netherlands	Spain
Passport/National Identity Card	●	●	●	●	●
Visa (regulations can change – check before planning your journey)	▲	▲	▲	▲	▲
Onward or return ticket	▲	▲	○	▲	▲
Health inoculations	▲	▲	▲	▲	▲
Travel insurance	○	○	○	○	○
Driving licence (national or international; Spain national only)	○	○	○	○	○
Health insurance	○	○	○	○	○
Health documentation	▲	▲	▲	▲	▲

WHEN TO GO

Lanzarote/Fuerteventura

High season
Low season

JAN	FEB	MAR	APR	MAY	JUN	JUL	AUG	SEP	OCT	NOV	DEC
21°C	21°C	23°C	24°C	25°C	26°C	28°C	29°C	29°C	27°C	24°C	21°C

☀ Sun

⛅ Sunshine & showers

TOURIST OFFICES

In the UK
Spanish National Tourist Office
79 New Cavendish Street
London W1W 6XB
☎ (020) 7486 8077
www.spain.info

In the USA
Spanish National Tourist Office
666 Fifth Ave, 35th floor
New York, NY 10103
☎ (212) 265-8822
www.okspain.org
Other SNTOs in Chicago, Los Angeles, Miami

In Canada
Spanish National Tourist Office
102 Bloor St W, Suite 3402
Toronto, Ontario
M4W 3E2
☎ (416) 961-3131
www.tourspain.toronto.on.ca

EMERGENCY SERVICES 112

WHEN YOU ARE THERE

ARRIVING

At Lanzarote All flights arrive at Arrecife airport (☎ 928 84 60 01), which lies between Arrecife and its main resort, Puerto del Carmen.

At Fuerteventura All flights arrive at Puerto del Rosario's small airport (☎ 928 86 06 04), which lies between the island's capital and Caleta de Fustes.

Arrecife Airport To Puerto del Carmen	Journey times	
	🚈	N/A
	🚌	20 minutes
10 kilometres	🚕	10 minutes

Puerto del Rosario Airport To Corralejo	Journey times	
	🚈	N/A
	🚌	1 hour
35 kilometres	🚕	45 minutes

MONEY

The euro (€) is the single currency of the European Monetary Union, which has been adopted by most member states including Spain and the Canary Islands. There are banknotes for 5, 10, 20, 50, 100, 200 and 500 euros, and coins for 1, 2, 5, 10, 20 and 50 cents, and 1 and 2 euros. ATMS (cash machines) can be found in all towns. Euro traveller's cheques are widely accepted. Spain's former currency, the peseta, is no longer accepted.

TIME

L Lanzarote and Fuerteventura (and all the Canaries) follow Greenwich Mean Time (GMT), but from the last Sunday in March – when clocks are put forward one hour – until the Saturday before the last Sunday in October, summer time operates (GMT+1).

CUSTOMS

 YES

As the Canaries are a free-trade zone there are no restrictions at all on the amounts of alcohol, tobacco, perfume and other goods that can be brought into the islands. It would be pointless to take most goods into these islands in the expectation of saving money, however: almost everything is cheaper in the Canaries than it is at home. Visitors may bring an unlimited amount of foreign currency but should declare any amount exceeding €6,000 in cash to avoid difficulties on leaving.

 NO

There are a few obvious exceptions to the above, notably drugs, firearms, obscene material and unlicensed animals.

CONSULATES

UK
Las Palmas, Gran
Canaria
☎ 928 26 25 08

Germany
Las Palmas, Gran
Canaria
☎ 928 49 18 80

USA
Las Palmas, Gran
Canaria
☎ 928 27 12 59

Netherlands
Las Palmas, Gran
Canaria
☎ 928 36 22 51

WHEN YOU ARE THERE

TOURIST OFFICES

In Lanzarote

● **Head office:**
Cabildo Insular de
Lanzarote
Consejería de Turismo
Patronato de Turismo
Blas Cabrera Felipe
35500 Arrecife
☎ 928 81 17 62
Fax: 928 80 00 80

● **Local offices:**
Arrecife: Airport ☎ 928 82
07 74
Muelle de los Mármoles,
☎ 928 80 13 26
Information kiosk in Parque
José Ramírez Cerdá,
☎ 928 81 31 74
Puerto del Carmen: beside
main beach, on Avenida de
las Playas ☎ 928 51 33 51
Playa Blanca: Calle
Varadero ☎ 928 51 90 18
Costa Teguise: CC Los
Charcos, Avenida Islas
Canarias, ☎ 928 82 71 30

In Fuerteventura

● **Head office:**
Patronato de Turismo de
Fuerteventura
Avenida Constitución 5
Puerto del Rosario
☎ 928 53 08 44

● **Local offices:**
Puerto del Rosario airport
☎ 928 86 06 04
Corralejo: La Oliva, Plaza
Pública ☎ 928 86 62 35
Caleta de Fuste: CC Castillo
Centro ☎ 928 16 32 86
Morro Jable: in the
shopping centre, Jandía
Beach ☎ 928 54 07 76

NATIONAL HOLIDAYS

J	F	M	A	M	J	J	A	S	O	N	D
2	1	1(1)	(1)	1(1)	(1)	1	1		1	1	3

1 January	Año Nuevo (New Year's Day)
6 January	Epifanía (Epiphany)
March/April	Pascua (Easter) Thu, Fri, Sun of Easter Week, and following Mon
1 May	Día del Trabajo (Labour Day)
30 May	Día de las Canarias
15 August	Asunción (Assumption)
12 October	Día de la Hispanidad (Columbus Day)
1 November	Día de Todos los Santos (All Saints' Day)
6 December	Día de la Constitucion (Constitution Day)
8 December	Inmaculada Concepción (Immaculate Conception)
25 December	Navidad (Christmas)

OPENING HOURS

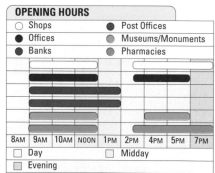

○ Shops   ● Post Offices
● Offices   ◐ Museums/Monuments
● Banks   ◐ Pharmacies

8AM	9AM	10AM	NOON	1PM	2PM	4PM	5PM	7PM

☐ Day   ☐ Midday
☐ Evening

In resorts, some shops keep longer hours and may
also be open on Sunday. Chemists keep similar hours
to other shops but are usually closed on Saturday
afternoons. At least one chemist per town is normally
open after hours. Many bars open for breakfast
around 7AM and stay open till about 1AM or later the
following morning. Even outside these hours you can
often find a bar open. Expect bars to be closed from
about 3AM–6AM. Museum opening times can be
unpredictable – many open in the mornings only.

**DRIVE ON THE
RIGHT**

**TOILETS
CHARGE**

PUBLIC TRANSPORT

 Flights Daily flights between Arrecife (Lanzarote) and Puerto del Rosario (Fuerteventura) take one hour and 50 minutes and are operated by Binter Canarias (☎ 902 39 13 92, www.binternet.com).

 Buses Public transport on the islands is mainly confined to a slow rural bus network designed to get villagers to and from the capital (Arrecife in Lanzarote, Puerto del Rosario in Fuerteventura), but there is a fast, frequent service between Lanzarote's resorts. Buses are always called by their local colloquial name, *guaguas* (pronounced wahwahs). Main bus station at Arrecife, Lanzarote: ☎ 928 81 15 22, www.arrecifebus.com; main bus station at Puerto del Rosario, Fuerteventura: ☎ 928 85 21 66, www.tiadhe.com.

 Ferries Between Lanzarote and Fuerteventura (and also to other Canary Islands) ferries are run by:
Trasmediterránea (in Arrecife, Lanzarote ☎ 928 81 11 74; in Puerto del Rosario, Fuerteventura ☎ 928 85 08 77)
Fred Olsen (Playa Blanca, Lanzarote ☎ 928 51 72 66; ticket office also at harbour in Corralejo, Fuerteventura ☎ 928 53 50 90)
Naviera Armas (Playa Blanca, Lanzarote ☎ 928 51 79 12; Calle José Antonio 90, Arrecife ☎ 928 82 49 30; the harbour at Corralejo, Fuerteventura ☎ 928 86 70 80).
To Isla de Lobos: Ferries Majorero (☎ 928 86 62 38), Isla de Lobos (no phone) and Celia Cruz (☎ 646 53 10 68) from Corralejo harbour, Fuerteventura
To Isla Graciosa: Ferry Líneas Romero from Orzola harbour, Lanzarote ☎ 928 84 20 70

CAR RENTAL

 Car hire is relatively cheap on Lanzarote, but dearer on Fuerteventura. Small local firms are efficient, though the (pricier) international firms are also represented. Minor roads on both islands are often little more than dirt tracks and signposting is sporadic.

TAXIS

 Cabs have a green 'for hire' light inside the windscreen, and a special SP licence plate ('*servicio público*'). Cabs are inexpensive (dearer on Fuerteventura than Lanzarote, though, simply because distances are longer).

DRIVING

 There are no motorways on these two islands.

 Speed limit on main roads: **100kph**

 Speed limit towns and villages: **40kph** unless indicated

 Seat belts are compulsory for all passengers. Children under 12 (excluding babies in rear-facing baby seats) must ride in the back seats.

 Driving under the influence of alcohol is strictly illegal, and consequences if involved in an accident will be severe, possibly including a jail term.

 Fuel is sold as *Sin plomo* (unleaded) and *Gasoleo* (diesel). Petrol stations are rare on both islands outside the capitals and the main resorts. Most service stations in the interior keep shop hours and don't always take credit cards.

 Lanzarote is notorious for accidents. If involved in a serious accident, call the emergency services on 112. If no one is injured, exchange details with other motorists involved. Hire cars and their drivers should all be insured by the hire company. Hire car companies should issue drivers with an emergency number to call in the event of a breakdown.

CENTIMETRES

ruler markings 0–8

INCHES

ruler markings 0–3

PERSONAL SAFETY

Crime is not a problem in Lanzarote and Fuerteventura. The greatest risk is theft by another tourist. Put all bags, clothes, etc, in the boot of your car where they cannot be seen, rather than on the back seat. If self-catering, lock all doors and windows before going out.

• Fire is a risk in hotels – locate the nearest fire exit to your room and ensure it is not blocked or locked.
• Do not leave possessions unattended on the beach or in cars.
• **In an emergency, call 112.** Otherwise call or visit the Guardia Civil (Arrecife: ☎ 928 59 21 00; Puerto del Rosario:
☎ 928 85 05 03)

TELEPHONES

All phone numbers in Spain, including the Canary Islands, have 9 digits, and you must dial the whole number. To use a public payphone, you'll usually need *a tarjeta de teléfono*, a phone card. These are

widely available from tobacconists and similar shops. To dial abroad first dial 00, wait for a change of tone, then dial the international code of the country you are calling (see below).

International dialling codes	
From the Canary Islands to:	
UK:	44
Germany:	49
USA & Canada:	1
Netherlands:	31
Mainland Spain:	9-digit number only

POST

Post boxes are yellow, and often have a slot marked 'Extranjeros' for mail to foreign countries.
Letters or cards to the UK cost 53 cents (up to 20g)
Postcards/letters to the US/Canada cost 78 cents (up to 20g)
Letters within Spain cost 28 cents. Post offices are open Mon–Fri 9–2, Sat 9–1.

ELECTRICITY

The voltage is 220/240v throughout both islands. Sockets take the standard

European two-round-pin plugs. Bring an adaptor for British or American appliances you wish to use with their usual plugs, and Americans should change the voltage setting on appliances.

TIPS/GRATUITIES

Yes ✓ No ✗		
Restaurants (service included)	✗	
Café	✓	nearest 50 cents
Taxi	✓	5–10%
Porter	✓	30–50 cents
Bar staff	✓	nearest 50 cents
Hairdressers	✓	€1–2
Cloakroom/washroom attn.	✓	a few cents
Tour guide	✓	€2
Room service	✓	€1

What To Photograph: Lanzarote's volcanic terrain, either as landscapes or in close up, provides extraordinary images of 'landscape as art'. Contrasts of black lava with dazzling white cottages are typical. Crops growing in black *picón* startle the eye. On Fuerteventura, immense dunescapes and beaches framed by sky and sea look like modern paintings.
Light: be aware of the intensity of light – photographing in the early morning or evening may give the best results.
Film: most popular brands are readily available at the resorts.

HEALTH

Insurance
Good medical health cover is essential in case of a medical emergency, although EU nationals receive free medical treatment with the relevant documentation (European Health Insurance Card (EHIC) for UK nationals). You may need to give a photocopy of the EHIC to the doctor. Hospital General de Lanzarote, Carretara Arrecife-Tinajo, tel 928 59 50 00. Hospital General de Fuerteventura, Carretera General de Aeropuerto, ☎ 928 86 20 93. German- and English-speaking doctors practise at Clinic Dr Mager, 37 Avenida de las Playas, Puerto del Carmen ☎ 928 51 26 11 (private clinic, form EHIC not accepted). There are also branches in Costa Teguise and Playa Blanca.

Dental Services
Emergency treatment may be expensive but is covered by most medical insurance (but not by form EHIC). Keep bills for insurance claims.

Sun Advice
The biggest danger to health here is overexposure to the sun. Not only are these islands most popular with North Europeans during the winter months when they are least accustomed to sun, but it is vital to remember that Lanzarote and Fuerteventura are 700 miles nearer the Equator than southern Spain, on the same latitude as the Sahara. Use generous amounts of high factor sun cream and avoid the sun at midday. A wide-brimmed hat and a T-shirt (even when swimming) are advisable for children.

Medication
Any essential medicines should be taken with you to Lanzarote or Fuerteventura. Most well-known proprietary brands of analgesics and popular remedies etc are available at all pharmacies. All medicines must be paid for, even if prescribed by a doctor.

Safe water
Tap water is safe all over the islands, except where signs indicate that water is not drinkable. However most water is desalinated and tastes unpleasant. Drink bottled water (*agua mineral*), sold either *sin gas* (still) or *con gas* (carbonated).

YOUTH CONCESSIONS

Lanzarote and Fuerteventura do not attract backpackers the way other holiday islands do. There are no youth hostels and few, if any, youth concessions available.

CLOTHING SIZES

Canary Islands	UK	Europe	USA		
46	36	46	36		Suits
48	38	48	38		
50	40	50	40		
52	42	52	42		
54	44	54	44		
56	46	56	46		
41	7	41	8		Shoes
42	7.5	42	8.5		
43	8.5	43	9.5		
44	9.5	44	10.5		
45	10.5	45	11.5		
46	11	46	12		
37	14.5	37	14.5		Shirts
38	15	38	15		
39/40	15.5	39/40	15.5		
41	16	41	16		
42	16.5	42	16.5		
40	17	40	17		
36	8	34	6		Dresses
38	10	36	8		
40	12	38	10		
42	14	40	12		
44	16	42	14		
46	18	44	16		
38	4.5	38	6		Shoes
38	5	38	6.5		
39	5.5	39	7		
39	6	39	7.5		
40	6.5	40	8		
41	7	41	8.5		

WHEN DEPARTING

- Always reconfirm your return flight with the airline or holiday rep at least one day before departing.
- Check in at least 2 hours before flight departure.
- Allow time to return your hire car.

LANGUAGE

People working in the tourist industry, including waiters, generally know some English. In places where few tourists venture, including bars and restaurants in Arrecife, it is helpful to know some basic Spanish.

Pronunciation guide: *b* almost like a *v*; *c* before *e* or *i* sounds like *th* otherwise like *k*; *d* can be like English *d* or like a *th*; *g* before *e* or *i* is a guttural *h*, between vowels like *h*, otherwise like *g*; *h* always silent; *j* guttural *h*; *ll* like English *lli* (as in 'million'); *ñ* sounds like *ni* in 'onion'; *qu* sound like *k*; *v* sounds a little like *b*; *z* like English *th*.

	hotel	*hotel*	breakfast	*el desayuno*
	room	*una habitación*	bathroom	*el cuarto de baño*
	single/double/	*individual/doble/*	shower	*la ducha*
	twin	*con dos camas*	balcony	*el balcón*
	one/two nights	*una noche/dos noches*	reception	*la recepción*
			key	*la llave*
	reservation	*una reserva*	room service	*el servicio de habitaciones*
	rate	*la tarifa*		

	bureau de change	*cambio*	pounds sterling	*la libra esterlina*
	post office	*correos*	US dollars	*dólares*
	cash machine/ ATM	*cajero automático*	banknote	*un billete de banco*
	foreign exchange	*cambio (de divisas)*	travellers' cheques	*cheques de viaje*
	foreign currency	*cambio*	credit card	*la tarjeta de crédito*

	restaurant	*restaurante*	cheers!	*salud!*
	cafe-bar	*bar*	dessert	*el postre*
	table	*una mesa*	water	*agua*
	menu	*la carta*	(house) wine	*vino (de la casa)*
	set menus	*platos combinados*	beer	*cerveza*
			drink	*la bebida*
	today's set menu	*el plato del día*	bill	*la cuenta*
	wine list	*la carta de vinos*	the toilet	*los servicios*

	plane	*el avion*	single/return...	*de ida / ...de ida y vuelta*
	airport	*el aeropuerto*		
	bus	*el autobús ('guagua')*	ticket office	*el despacho de billetes*
	ferry	*el ferry*	timetable	*el horario*
	terminal	*terminus*	seat	*un asiento*
	ticket	*un billete*	reserved seat	*un asiento reservado*

yes	*si*	is there..?, do you have..?	*hay...?*
no	*no*		
please	*por favor*	I don't speak Spanish	*No hablo español*
thank you	*gracias*		
hello/hi	*hola!*	I am ...	*Soy ...*
hello/good day	*buenos dias*	I have ..	*Tengo ...*
sorry, pardon me	*perdon*	help!	*socorro!*
bye, see you	*hasta luego*	how much	*cuánto es?*
that's fine	*está bien*	open	*abierto*
what?	*como?*	closed	*cerrado*

Acknowledgements
The Automobile Assocation wishes to thank the following photographers, libraries and
associations for their assistance in the preparation of this book:
MARY EVANS PICTURE LIBRARY 10; MUSEO DE HISTORIA DE TENERIFE 11; NATURE
PHOTOGRAPHERS LTD 86b (Brinsley Burbidge); www.euro.ecb.int/ 119 (euro notes).

The remaining photographs are held in the Association's own photo library (AA PHOTO LIBRARY)
and were taken by S DAY, except the following:
C SAWYER 7b, 7c, 15b, 16b, 17b, 23b, 24b, 36/7, 41b, 47b, 50/1, 55b, 64, 65, 66/7, 68b, 69a, 69b,
71b, 82b, 83a; JA TIMS 73b, 122a, 122b, 122c.

Updated by Joanne Williams

Dear Essential Traveller

Your comments, opinions and recommendations are very important to us. So please help us to improve our travel guides by taking a few minutes to complete this simple questionnaire.

You do not need a stamp (unless posted outside the UK). If you do not want to cut this page from your guide, then photocopy it or write your answers on a plain sheet of paper.

Send to: **The Editor, AA World Travel Guides, FREEPOST SCE 4598, Basingstoke RG21 4GY.**

Your recommendations...

We always encourage readers' recommendations for restaurants, nightlife or shopping – if your recommendation is used in the next edition of the guide, we will send you a *FREE* **AA** *Essential* **Guide** of your choice. Please state below the establishment name, location and your reasons for recommending it.

_____

_____

_____

_____

Please send me **AA** *Essential* _____

About this guide...

Which title did you buy?

AA *Essential* _____

Where did you buy it? _____   _____

When? m m / y y

Why did you choose an AA *Essential* Guide? _____

_____

_____

_____

Did this guide meet your expectations?

Exceeded ☐   Met all ☐   Met most ☐   Fell below ☐

Please give your reasons_____

_____

_____

_____

continued on next page...

Were there any aspects of this guide that you particularly liked? _____

_____

_____

Is there anything we could have done better? _____

_____

_____

About you...

Name (*Mr/Mrs/Ms*) _____

Address _____

_____

_____ Postcode _____

Daytime tel nos _____

Please only give us your mobile phone number if you wish to hear from us
about other products and services from the AA and partners by text or mms.

Which age group are you in?
 Under 25 ☐ 25–34 ☐ 35–44 ☐ 45–54 ☐ 55–64 ☐ 65+ ☐

How many trips do you make a year?
 Less than one ☐ One ☐ Two ☐ Three or more ☐

Are you an AA member? Yes ☐ No ☐

About your trip...

When did you book? m m / y y   When did you travel? m m / y y
How long did you stay? _____
Was it for business or leisure? _____
Did you buy any other travel guides for your trip?
 If yes, which ones? _____

Thank you for taking the time to complete this questionnaire. Please send it to us as soon as
possible, and remember, you do not need a stamp (*unless posted outside the UK*).

Happy Holidays!

The information we hold about you will be used to provide the products and services requested
and for identification, account administration, analysis, and fraud/loss prevention purposes. More
details about how that information is used is in our privacy statement, which you'll find under the
heading "Personal Information" in our terms and conditions and on our website: www.theAA.com.
Copies are also available from us by post, by contacting the Data Protection Manager at AA, Fanum
House, Basing View, Basingstoke, Hampshire RG21 4EA.

We may want to contact you about other products and services provided by us, or our partners (by
mail, telephone) but please tick the box if you DO NOT wish to hear about such products and
services from us by mail or telephone. ☐